Assessment Book

Level D

Editorial Offices: Glenview, Illinois • Parsippany, New Jersey
New York, New York
Sales Offices: Boston, Massachusetts • Duluth, Georgia
Glenview, Illinois • Coppell, Texas • Sacramento, California • Mesa, Arizona

0-328-21395-0

8 9 10 V031 15 14 13 12 11 10 09 08

CC1

Table of Contents

Distinctions Between Levels

Understanding the Levels of *My Sidewalks*

The goal of the *My Sidewalks* program is to enable struggling readers to succeed with the reading material used in their regular classrooms. To achieve this, *My Sidewalks* focuses on accelerating students' acquisition of priority skills. Each level of *My Sidewalks* is designed to provide a year and a half of reading growth. Consequently there is an overlap of skills between one *My Sidewalks* level and the next.

These pages describe the skills students should have to successfully begin each level of *My Sidewalks* and what they will learn in that level. Use the Placement Tests to help you determine the correct level at which to enter each student.

To begin this level a child should know:	**In this level**, the instructional focus is on:
Early Reading Intervention (Grade K)	
	• Phonological and phonemic awareness • Letter names and sounds • Blending regular short-vowel words • Sentence reading
Level A (Grade 1)	
• Some phonological awareness	• Phonemic awareness • Letter names • Consonants: Individual letter-sounds, blends, and digraphs • Vowels: Short, long (CVCe), and *r*-controlled • Blending words and fluent word reading • High-frequency words • Oral vocabulary and concept development • Building fluency (40–60 WCPM) • Passage reading and retelling

To begin this level a student should know:	In this level, the instructional focus is on:

Level B (Grade 2)

- Letter names - Individual consonant letter-sounds - Some basic high-frequency words - And be able to read Benchmark Reader A2 with accuracy and comprehension	- Phonemic awareness - Letter names and sounds - Blending words and fluent word reading - High-frequency words - Oral vocabulary and concept development - Building fluency (70–90 wcpm) - Passage reading and retelling

Level C (Grade 3)

- Consonants: Individual letter-sounds, blends, and digraphs - Vowels: Short and long (CVCe) and be able to distinguish between them - A wider range of high-frequency words - And be able to read Benchmark Reader B2 with accuracy and comprehension	- Blending words and fluent word reading - Decoding multisyllabic words, including words with one or more affixes - Phonics: Vowels - Concept vocabulary - Building fluency (100–120 wcpm) - Passage reading and summarizing

Level D (Grade 4)

- Consonants: Individual letter-sounds, blends, and digraphs - Vowels: Short and long (CVCe) and be able to distinguish between them - How to decode regular VC/CV words with short and long (CVCe) vowels - Many high-frequency words - And be able to read Benchmark Reader C1 with accuracy and comprehension	- Decoding multisyllabic words, including words with one or more affixes - Phonics: Less frequent vowel patterns, such as vowel diphthongs - Concept vocabulary - Building fluency (110–130 wcpm) - Passage reading and summarizing

Level E (Grade 5)

- Consonants: Individual letter-sounds, blends, and digraphs - Vowels: Short and long (CVCe) and be able to distinguish between them - How to decode regular VC/CV words with short and long (CVCe) vowels - Many high-frequency words - And be able to read Benchmark Reader D1 with accuracy and comprehension	- Decoding multisyllabic words, including words with one or more affixes - Phonics: Less frequent vowel patterns, such as vowel diphthongs - Concept vocabulary - Building fluency (120–140 wcpm) - Passage reading and summarizing

Differentiating Instruction

The charts on these pages show instruction during a week in *My Sidewalks*. The charts can also be used as guides for **reteaching** or **accelerating** through parts of the lessons.

In addition, the *If... then...* directions will help you identify how to customize instruction for your students.

Reteaching To meet the needs of the lowest performing readers, it may be necessary to modify the pacing and intensity of instruction. Activities shown in gray boxes on the charts may be repeated for these students.

Accelerating A child who shows mastery of skills following initial instruction may be ready for instruction at a faster pace with fewer repetitions. Activities shown in light gray boxes might be omitted for these students.

Levels A–B

	PHONEMIC AWARENESS	PHONICS	HIGH-FREQUENCY WORDS	CONCEPTS/ ORAL VOCABULARY	PASSAGE READING	FLUENCY	WRITING
Day 1	Phonemic Awareness	Blending Strategy	High-Frequency Words	Concepts/ Oral Vocabulary	Read a Passage	Reread for Fluency	
Day 2	Phonemic Awareness	Blending Strategy	High-Frequency Words		Read a Passage	Reread for Fluency	Write
Day 3	Phonemic Awareness	Blending Strategy	High-Frequency Words	Concepts/ Oral Vocabulary	Read a Passage	Reread for Fluency	
Day 4		Fluent Word Reading		Concepts/ Oral Vocabulary	Read Together	Reread for Fluency	Write
Day 5		Assess Word Reading	Assess Word/ Sentence Reading	Check Oral Vocabulary	Assess Passage Reading/ Reread		Write

▨ **Reteach**   ▨ **Omit for acceleration**

If... a child is struggling with word reading, *then...* reteach Word Work activities and include More Practice extensions.

If... a child lacks oral language, *then...* elicit extended language from the child, provide ample opportunities for the child to respond when building concepts, and expand the structured picture walks before reading each selection.

If... a child's reading is so slow that it hinders comprehension, *then...* provide additional models of fluent reading, give more corrective feedback during fluency practice, and include More Practice extensions when rereading for fluency.

If... an English learner struggles with sounds, *then...* repeat appropriate practice activities.

Levels C–E

	VOCABULARY	COMPRE-HENSION	PASSAGE READING	PHONICS	FLUENCY	WRITING
Day 1	Vocabulary		Read a Passage	Blending Strategy (Level C)	Reread for Fluency	Write (Levels D–E)
Day 2	Vocabulary	Comprehension Skill	Read a Passage	Phonics	Reread for Fluency	Write (Levels D–E)
Day 3	Vocabulary	Comprehension Skill Assess (Levels D–E)	Read a Passage	Phonics	Reread for Fluency	Write
Day 4	Vocabulary	Comprehension Skill/Strategy Assess (Levels D–E)	Read Together (Level C) Read a Passage (Levels D–E)	Phonics Review (Level C)	Reread for Fluency	Write
Day 5	Vocabulary	Assess Comprehension	Read Together (Levels D–E) Reread (Level C)	Assess Sentence Reading (Level C)	Assess Fluency	Write

If... a student is struggling with word reading, **then...** reteach Vocabulary and Phonics activities and include More Practice extensions.

If... a student lacks oral language, **then...** elicit extended language from the student, provide ample opportunities for the student to respond when building concepts, and expand the After Reading discussion for each selection.

If... a student's reading is so disfluent that it hinders comprehension, **then...** provide additional models of fluent reading, give more corrective feedback during fluency practice, and include More Practice extensions for fluency.

If... a student lacks comprehension and is unable to retell or summarize, **then...** reteach comprehension skills and strategies, provide additional modeling of retelling and summarizing, and give more corrective feedback during practice.

If... an English learner lacks English vocabulary for known concepts, **then...** say the unknown English word, have the student repeat it, and ask questions that will allow the student to use the word in a meaningful context.

My Sidewalks, Level D Intensive Reading Intervention

Assessment Plan

4-Step Plan for Assessment

1 Diagnosis and Placement
2 Monitor Progress
3 Evaluate Student Progress
4 Exiting the Program

The assessments in this handbook will enable you to gather valuable information about your students' understanding and mastery of reading skills before, during, and after instruction.

Step 1 Diagnosis and Placement

Use the Placement Test with individual at-risk students who have been identified through baseline test performance, work in the core reading program, and observation. Administer the *My Sidewalks* Placement Test to determine the level at which to begin students in *My Sidewalks* and to identify the areas of literacy (word reading, fluency, or comprehension) that are problematic for each student.

Placement Test Overview

The Level D Placement Test is designed to help you identify the appropriate level at which to begin students who will use *My Sidewalks*. The four subtests are to be administered with individual at-risk students who have been identified through baseline test performance, work in the core reading program, and observation. The chart below shows the number of items in each subtest. Estimated times are given for planning purposes only. Allow as much time as needed for each student to complete the test. You may administer this test in two or three sittings.

Subtest	Number of Items	Estimated Time
1 Word Reading: Phonics	20	1 minute
2 Word Reading: High-Frequency Words	20	1 minute
3 Fluency and Comprehension	wcpm Retelling	12 minutes
4 Word Reading: Benchmark Words	20	1 minute
Total	80	15 minutes

Directions for Administering the Test

Directions for each subtest appear on pp. 20–21. The directions in **bold** type are to be read aloud.

Make two copies of the student's test, pp. 22–23, one for the student and one for you to mark. Also make a copy of the Evaluation Chart, p. 19, for each student. Have Benchmark Reader C6 on hand. For your convenience, the Level C Benchmark Readers are reproduced on pp. 112–122.

Begin with Subtests 1–2. If the student scores less than 80% on Subtests 1–2, discontinue testing. If the student scores 80% or better on Subtests 1–2, continue testing.

Scoring

Record each student's scores on a copy of the Evaluation Chart. There is an Answer Key on pp. 124–128.

Interpreting the Scores

- If the student scores less than 80% on Subtests 1–2, he or she may be more appropriately placed in Level C of *My Sidewalks* or may require further testing.
- Students who score 80% or better on Subtests 1–2 and who can read the Subtest 3 passage with 95% accuracy and retell with a summative score of 2 are appropriately placed in Level D of *My Sidewalks*.
- Students who score above 90% on Subtests 1–2 and who read and retell the Subtest 3 passage accurately should continue with Subtest 4. Students who score 80% or better on Subtest 4 should be asked to read Benchmark Reader C6. Students who read Benchmark Reader C6 with 90% accuracy, at a rate of approximately 100 wcsw, and have a summative retelling score of 3 may be capable of working in a core fourth-grade reading program with instructional emphasis in the areas of need and with strategic intervention.

18   Placement Test Overview

Step 2 Monitor Progress

Use the ongoing assessments found on Day 5 each week in the Teacher's Guides to identify individual instructional needs and to provide appropriate support. Use retellings and the Fluency Progress Chart found in the Teacher's Guides to track each student's progress.

Level D1 Benchmark Reader

Step 3 Evaluate Student Progress

Administer the Unit Tests to check mastery of unit skills. To make instructional decisions at the end of a unit, use end-of-unit assessment results, which include students' performance on Day 5 assessments for that unit, on the Unit Test, and on reading of the unit Benchmark Reader. (Use of the Benchmark Reader is optional.) Use the Fluency Progress Chart on p. 11, the Retelling Progress Chart on p. 14, and the Record Chart for Unit Tests on p. 16 to gather complete end-of-unit information.

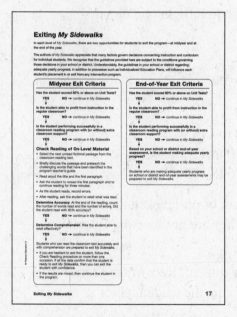

Step 4 Exiting the Program

There are two opportunities for students to exit the program—at midyear and at the end of the year. To exit the program, a student must show progress toward grade-level goals. Use the Midyear and End-of-Year Exit Criteria on p. 17 as your guide.

Monitoring Fluency

Ongoing assessment of reading fluency is one of the most valuable measures we have of students' reading skills. One of the most effective ways to assess fluency is taking timed samples of students' oral reading and measuring the number of words correct per minute (WCPM).

How to Assess Fluency

Make one copy of the fluency passage for yourself and one for the student to read. Fluency passages are provided for use in the Unit Tests. Say to the student: **As you read this aloud, I want you to do your best reading and to read as quickly as you can. That doesn't mean it's a race. Just do your best, fast reading. When I say** *begin,* **start reading.**

As the student reads, follow along in your copy. Mark words that are read incorrectly. Explanations of these miscues are found in the Teacher's Guides, Volumes 1 and 2, on page 192.

Incorrect
- omissions
- substitutions
- mispronunciations
- insertions

Correct
- self-corrections within 3 seconds
- repeated words

At the end of one minute, draw a line after the last word that was read. Have the student finish reading, but don't count any words beyond one minute. Arrive at the words correct per minute—WCPM—by counting the total number of words that the student read correctly in one minute.

Fluency Goals

Level D End-of-Year Goal = 110–130 WCPM

Target Goals by Unit

Unit 1 60 to 80 WCPM	**Unit 4** 90 to 110 WCPM
Unit 2 70 to 90 WCPM	**Unit 5** 100 to 120 WCPM
Unit 3 80 to 100 WCPM	**Unit 6** 110 to 130 WCPM

Note: The fluency goals at the high end of the range are more typical of on-level students, and students in intensive intervention may be progressing well even if they are not meeting fluency benchmarks.

Fluency Progress Chart Copy the chart on the next page for each student. Record the score for each timed reading by coloring in the column up to that point or having the student color it.

Student's Name _____

Fluency Progress Chart

Level D Fluency Goals
Midyear Goal: 80–100 WCPM
End-of-Year Goal: 110–130 WCPM

Level D Fluency Progress Chart

Words Correct per Minute (WCPM)	END-OF-UNIT 1	UNIT 1 BENCHMARK READER	END-OF-UNIT 2	UNIT 2 BENCHMARK READER	END-OF-UNIT 3	UNIT 3 BENCHMARK READER	END-OF-UNIT 4	UNIT 4 BENCHMARK READER	END-OF-UNIT 5	UNIT 5 BENCHMARK READER	END-OF-UNIT 6	UNIT 6 BENCHMARK READER
140												
135												
130												
125												
120												
115												
110												
105												
100												
95												
90												
85												
80												
75												
70												
65												
60												
55												
50												

Unit Test_____   Benchmark Reader_____
(Mark one.)

Narrative Retelling Scoring Rubric and Chart

If students have difficulty retelling, then use these prompts.
- Who is this story about? Tell me more about _____.
- Where or when does the story take place?
- What happens in the beginning of the story? in the middle? at the end?

Narrative Retelling Scoring Rubric			
Score	**3**	**2**	**1**
Characters	Identifies the main characters and adds details about each	Identifies the main characters without providing details	Is unable to distinguish the main characters
Setting	Identifies the time and location	Omits details of time or location	Does not identify time or location
Plot	Accurately describes the beginning, middle, and end of the story	Retells parts of the story with gaps that affect meaning	Retelling has no sense of story

Note No score indicates no response.

Narrative Retelling Chart			
Retelling Criteria	**Teacher-Aided Response**	**Student-Generated Response**	**Rubric Score (Circle one.)**
Characters			3 2 1
Setting			3 2 1
Plot			3 2 1

Record the Summative Score on the student's Record Sheet for Unit Tests and/or Retelling Progress Chart.

Summative Score Guidelines		
3 Rubric Score of all 3s in all Retelling Criteria	**2** Rubric Score of 3s, 2s, and some 1s in all Retelling Criteria	**1** Rubric Score of 1s or no response in all Retelling Criteria
Summative Score (Circle one.)	3 2 1	

Student's Name _____   Level D Unit _____

Unit Test_____   Benchmark Reader_____
(Mark one.)

Expository Retelling Scoring Rubric and Chart

If students have difficulty retelling, then use these prompts.
- What is this selection mostly about?
- What is important to know about _____?
- What did you learn about _____?

Expository Retelling Scoring Rubric			
Score	**3**	**2**	**1**
Topic	Identifies the main topic with some details	Identifies the main topic with no details	Does not identify the main topic
Important Ideas	Identifies main ideas	Gives limited information about main ideas	Does not identify any main ideas or gives inaccurate information about ideas
Conclusions	Draws defensible conclusions about the text	Draws conclusions about the text with limited support	Draws inaccurate or no conclusions about the text

Note No score indicates no response.

Expository Retelling Chart			
Retelling Criteria	**Teacher-Aided Response**	**Student-Generated Response**	**Rubric Score (Circle one.)**
Topic			3 2 1
Important Ideas			3 2 1
Conclusions			3 2 1

Record the Summative Score on the student's Record Sheet for Unit Tests and/or
Retelling Progress Chart.

Summative Score Guidelines		
3 Rubric Score of all 3s in all Retelling Criteria	**2** Rubric Score of 3s, 2s, and some 1s in all Retelling Criteria	**1** Rubric Score of 1s or no response in all Retelling Criteria
Summative Score (Circle one.)	3 2 1	

Retelling Progress Chart

Fill in the student's scores for each retelling (comprehension assessment) completed.

Date	Assessment	Narrative			Expository			
		Characters	Setting	Plot	Topic	Important Ideas	Conclusions	Summative Score
	Unit 1 Unit Test							
	Unit 1 Benchmark Reader							
	Unit 2 Unit Test							
	Unit 2 Benchmark Reader							
	Unit 3 Unit Test							
	Unit 3 Benchmark Reader							
	Unit 4 Unit Test							
	Unit 4 Benchmark Reader							
	Unit 5 Unit Test							
	Unit 5 Benchmark Reader							

© Pearson Education D

My Sidewalks, Level D
Intensive Reading Intervention

Using Benchmark Readers

There is one Benchmark Reader for each unit in *My Sidewalks*. The Benchmark Readers can serve as alternative tools for assessment. Benchmark Readers may be used

- to help determine a student's appropriate placement in *My Sidewalks*
- to measure a student's fluency (WCPM) and comprehension (retelling)
- to assess a student's mastery of phonics skills and high-frequency words for a completed unit, using connected text
- to confirm readiness for starting a new unit

Each Benchmark Reader utilizes the target phonics skills for the unit. Examples of the phonics skills are listed on the inside back cover of the book, along with a word count for measuring words correct per minute. Suggested retelling prompts and the Scoring Rubrics for Retelling on pages 12–13 can be used to assess a student's comprehension of the text.

**Level D1
Benchmark Reader**

**Level D2
Benchmark Reader**

**Level D3
Benchmark Reader**

**Level D4
Benchmark Reader**

**Level D5
Benchmark Reader**

**Level D6
Benchmark Reader**

Record Chart for Unit Tests

		Score		Reteach ✔	Individual Retest Score	Comments
		Individual	Group			
Unit 1	Word Reading: Phonics	/35	/10		/35	
	Concept Vocabulary	/25	/5		/25	
	Fluency WCPM					
	Retelling Score					
	Comprehension		/5			
Unit 2	Word Reading: Phonics	/30	/10		/30	
	Concept Vocabulary	/25	/5		/25	
	Fluency WCPM					
	Retelling Score					
	Comprehension		/5			
Unit 3	Word Reading: Phonics	/35	/10		/35	
	Concept Vocabulary	/25	/5		/25	
	Fluency WCPM					
	Retelling Score					
	Comprehension		/5			
Unit 4	Word Reading: Phonics	/30	/10		/30	
	Concept Vocabulary	/25	/5		/25	
	Fluency WCPM					
	Retelling Score					
	Comprehension		/5			
Unit 5	Word Reading: Phonics	/30	/10		/30	
	Concept Vocabulary	/25	/5		/25	
	Fluency WCPM					
	Retelling Score					
	Comprehension		/5			
Unit 6	Word Reading: Phonics	/30	/10		/30	
	Concept Vocabulary	/25	/5		/25	
	Fluency WCPM					
	Retelling Score					
	Comprehension		/5			

Record Scores Use this chart to record scores for the Level D Unit Tests.

Reteach Reteach phonics skills or provide additional practice with concept words if the student scores below 80% on either portion of the Unit Test.

Retest The Individual Unit Test may be used to retest skills that have been retaught.

To move into the next unit of *My Sidewalks*, students should	The student may be more appropriately placed in *My Sidewalks* Level C if
• score 80% or better on the Unit Test	• the student makes little progress in Unit 1, scoring 60% or lower on the Unit 1 Test
• be able to read and retell the end-of-unit Benchmark Reader accurately	• and is struggling to keep up with the Level D group
• be capable of working in the Level D group based on teacher judgment	• and, based on teacher judgment, the Level D materials are not at the student's level

© Pearson Education D

Exiting *My Sidewalks*

In each level of *My Sidewalks*, there are two opportunities for students to exit the program—at midyear and at the end of the year.

The authors of *My Sidewalks* appreciate that many factors govern decisions concerning instruction and curriculum for individual students. We recognize that the guidelines provided here are subject to the conditions governing those decisions in your school or district. Understandably, the guidelines in your school or district regarding adequate yearly progress, in addition to processes such as Individualized Education Plans, will influence each student's placement in or exit from any intervention program.

Midyear Exit Criteria

Has the student scored 80% or above on Unit Tests?

YES   **NO →** continue in *My Sidewalks*

Is the student able to profit from instruction in the regular classroom?

YES   **NO →** continue in *My Sidewalks*

Is the student performing successfully in a classroom reading program with (or without) extra classroom support?

YES   **NO →** continue in *My Sidewalks*

Check Reading of On-Level Material

- Select the next unread fictional passage from the classroom reading text.
- Briefly discuss the passage and preteach the challenging words that have been identified in the program teacher's guide.
- Read aloud the title and the first paragraph.
- Ask the student to reread the first paragraph and to continue reading for three minutes.
- As the student reads, record errors.
- After reading, ask the student to retell what was read.

Determine Accuracy At the end of the reading, count the number of words read and the number of errors. Did the student read with 85% accuracy?

YES   **NO →** continue in *My Sidewalks*

Determine Comprehension Was the student able to retell effectively?

YES   **NO →** continue in *My Sidewalks*

Students who can read the classroom text accurately and with comprehension are prepared to exit *My Sidewalks*.

- If you are hesitant to exit the student, follow the Check Reading procedure on more than one occasion. If all the data confirm that the student is ready to exit *My Sidewalks*, then you can exit the student with confidence.
- If the results are mixed, then continue the student in the program.

End-of-Year Exit Criteria

Has the student scored 80% or above on Unit Tests?

YES   **NO →** continue in *My Sidewalks*

Is the student able to profit from instruction in the regular classroom?

YES   **NO →** continue in *My Sidewalks*

Is the student performing successfully in a classroom reading program with (or without) extra classroom support?

YES   **NO →** continue in *My Sidewalks*

Based on your school or district end-of-year assessment, is the student making adequate yearly progress?

YES   **NO →** continue in *My Sidewalks*

Students who are making adequate yearly progress on school or district end-of-year assessments may be prepared to exit *My Sidewalks*.

Placement Test Overview

The Level D Placement Test is designed to help you identify the appropriate level at which to begin students who will use *My Sidewalks*. The four subtests are to be administered with individual at-risk students who have been identified through baseline test performance, work in the core reading program, and observation. The chart below shows the number of items in each subtest. Estimated times are given for planning purposes only. Allow as much time as needed for each student to complete the test. You may administer this test in two or three sittings.

Subtest	Number of Items	Estimated Time
1 Word Reading: Phonics	20	1 minute
2 Word Reading: High-Frequency Words	20	1 minute
3 Fluency and Comprehension	WCPM Retelling	12 minutes
4 Word Reading: Benchmark Words	20	1 minute
Total	**60**	**15 minutes**

Directions for Administering the Test

Directions for each subtest appear on pp. 20–21. The directions in **bold** type are to be read aloud.

Make two copies of the student's test, pp. 22–23, one for the student and one for you to mark. Also make a copy of the Evaluation Chart, p. 19, for each student. Have Benchmark Reader C6 on hand. For your convenience, the Level C Benchmark Readers are reproduced on pp. 112–122.

Begin with Subtests 1–2. If the student scores less than 80% on Subtests 1–2, discontinue testing. If the student scores 80% or better on Subtests 1–2, continue testing.

Scoring

Record each student's scores on a copy of the Evaluation Chart. There is an Answer Key on pp. 124–128.

Interpreting the Scores

- If the student scores less than 80% on Subtests 1–2, he or she may be more appropriately placed in Level C of *My Sidewalks* or may require further testing.

- Students who score 80% or better on Subtests 1–2 and who can read the Subtest 3 passage with 95% accuracy and retell with a summative score of 2 are appropriately placed in Level D of *My Sidewalks*.

- Students who score above 90% on Subtests 1–2 and who read and retell the Subtest 3 passage accurately should continue with Subtest 4. Students who score 80% or better on Subtest 4 should be asked to read Benchmark Reader C6. Students who read Benchmark Reader C6 with 90% accuracy, at a rate of approximately 100 WCPM, and who have a summative retelling score of 3 may be capable of working in a core fourth-grade reading program with instructional emphasis in the areas of need and with strategic intervention.

© Pearson Education D

Evaluation Chart

1 Word Reading: Phonics

SCORE SUBTEST 1	_____ / 20

2 Word Reading: High-Frequency Words

SCORE SUBTEST 2	_____ / 20

3a Fluency

_____ WCPM

3b Comprehension: Narrative Retelling

Retelling Criteria	Rubric Score		
Characters	3	2	1
Setting	3	2	1
Plot	3	2	1
SUMMATIVE SCORE	_____ / 3		

4 Word Reading: Benchmark Words

SCORE SUBTEST 4	_____ / 20

SCORE TOTALS

1 Word Reading: Phonics	_____ / 20
2 Word Reading: High-Frequency Words	_____ / 20
TOTAL SCORE	_____ / 40

Note: Subtest 4 is not part of the Placement Test for most students.

4 Word Reading: Benchmark Words	_____ / 20

PERCENTAGES

	Total Score: Subtests 1–2	Subtest 4
100%	40	20
90%	36	18
80%	32	16

Placement Test

1 Word Reading: Phonics

Display student test page 22. Say

- **Read the words in part 1 aloud. Begin next to the number 1, and read across the line. Read all four lines. Stop when you get to the end of part 1.**

Mark correct responses on your copy of the test page. Record the number correct on the Evaluation Chart.

2 Word Reading: High-Frequency Words

Display student test page 22. Say

- **Read the words in part 2 aloud. Begin next to the number 2, and read across the line. Read all four lines. Stop when you get to the end of part 2.**

Mark correct responses on your copy of the test page. Record the number correct on the Evaluation Chart.

3 Fluency and Comprehension

Assess Fluency Display student test page 23. Say

- **Now I will ask you to read a story aloud to me.**
- **Use your best reading as you read this story titled "My Friends, the Jugglers."**

As the student reads orally, mark any errors on your copy of the text. Stop the student at exactly one minute, and note precisely where the student stopped. Count the total number of words the student read in a minute. Subtract the number of words the student read incorrectly. Record the words correct per minute (WCPM) score on the Evaluation Chart.

Assess Comprehension Have the student reread the story on page 23 quietly. Say

- **Now I want you to read the story quietly to yourself.**
- **When you finish reading, I will ask you to tell me about what you read.**
- **Now read about the friends who are jugglers.**

When the student has finished, ask

- **Who is the story about? Tell me more about these characters.**
- **Where and when does the story take place?**
- **What happens in the beginning of the story? in the middle? at the end?**

Use the Narrative Retelling Scoring Rubric that follows to evaluate the student's retelling. Record the Summative Score on the Evaluation Chart.

Summative Score Guidelines		
3 Rubric Score of all 3s in all Retelling Criteria	2 Rubric Score of 3s, 2s, and some 1s in all Retelling Criteria	1 Rubric Score of 1s or no response in all Retelling Criteria

Narrative Retelling Scoring Rubric			
Score	3	2	1
Characters	Identifies the main characters and adds details about each	Identifies the main characters without providing details	Is unable to distinguish the main characters
Setting	Identifies the time and location	Omits details of time or location	Does not identify time or location
Plot	Accurately describes the beginning, middle, and end of the story	Retells parts of the story with gaps that affect meaning	Retelling has no sense of story

Note No score indicates no response.

4 Word Reading: Benchmark Words

This subtest should be given after Subtest 3 only to students who scored above 90% on Subtests 1–2 and who read and retold the Subtest 3 passage with a high degree of accuracy.

Display student test page 22. Say

- **Read the words in part 4 aloud. Begin next to the number 4, and read across the line. Read all four lines. Stop when you get to the end of part 4.**

Mark correct responses on your copy of the test page. Record the number correct on the Evaluation Chart. If the student scored 80% or better on Subtest 4, then ask the student to read Benchmark Reader C6 aloud. Use the Subtest 3 directions to evaluate the student's reading of Benchmark Reader C6.

1

shack	drove	fifth	sketch	flute
comment	cactus	product	hundred	impress
shake	tadpole	confuse	invites	translate
pinches	asking	bodies	intended	scrubbed

2

family	every	people	their	different
laugh	machine	picture	clothes	important
above	should	change	leave	beautiful
heard	country	build	special	America

3 Passage Reading

4

gnat	search	midnight	preheat	chemist
instead	violent	applaud	daughter	overjoyed
shrewdly	cruiser	signature	reservation	neighborhood
decision	governor	additional	cheerfulness	intelligent

Placement Test

3 My Friends, the Jugglers

Do you know how to juggle? The other day I saw my friends   13

Mack and Jackie in the park downtown. They were juggling! They   24

each had three balls. The balls were purple and orange.   34

Mack said it takes a lot of practice to juggle. It is difficult to   48

move three objects in a circular motion with only two hands.   59

You have to concentrate. After a while, you get into a rhythm.   71

"Show me how!" I requested. Jackie and Mack started by   81

tossing one ball up into the air. They quickly followed with a   93

second ball and then a third! My eyes tried to follow the pattern.   106

The balls kept moving in the same direction. As my friends moved   118

their arms, they continued to keep their eyes on the balls.   129

It was incredible. Now they are trying to juggle four balls at   141

one time. I hope they can teach me how to juggle too.   153

Level D—Unit 1

My Sidewalks offers two assessment options for each unit: a one-on-one Individual Test and a Group Test. Use just one of these options with your students. The Individual Test is the preferred option for use with intervention students since it will give you more precise information about their reading skills. You do not need to administer both tests.

Option 1 Individual Test

Directions This test is to be administered one-on-one to individual students. Make two copies of the test on page 26 and of the fluency passage on page 29, one for the student and one for you to mark. Read aloud the directions in **bold**.

- **This is a test about reading. In the first part, you will read a story aloud to me.**

Part One Fluency and Comprehension

Assess Fluency Take a one-minute sample of the student's oral reading of the passage on page 29.

- **I am going to ask you to read a story aloud to me.**
- **Use your best reading as you read this story titled "Let's Go Spelunking!"**

Have the student read aloud for one minute. Note miscues on your copy. After testing, record the words correct per minute (WCPM) on the Fluency Progress Chart on page 11.

Assess Comprehension Have the student read the story quietly. If the student has difficulty with the passage, you may read it aloud.

- **Now I want you to read the story quietly to yourself.**
- **When you finish reading, I will ask you to tell me about what you read.**
- **Now read about spelunking.**

When the student has finished, or when you have finished reading it aloud, ask

- **Who is this story about? Tell me more about Ann.**
- **Where or when does the story take place?**
- **What is the problem or goal? How is the problem solved or the goal reached?**

Use the Narrative Retelling Scoring Rubric on page 12 to evaluate the student's retelling.

Part Two Phonics Words

Assess Phonics Skills Use the words at the top of page 26 to assess the student's ability to read words with this unit's phonics skills. Have each student read the words aloud. Mark errors on your copy. Record the student's score on the Word Reading Chart on page 34.

- **Now I'm going to ask you to read some words aloud to me.**
- **Point to the number 1 at the top of this page.**
- **Use your best reading to read the words in row 1.**

Continue in the same way for rows 2–5.

Part Three Phonics Sentences

Assess Phonics Skills Use the sentences in the middle of page 26 to assess the student's ability to read sentences with this unit's phonics skills. Have each student read the sentences aloud. Listen for the student's pronunciation of the phonics word in **bold** in each sentence. Mark errors on your copy. Record the student's score on the Word Reading Chart on page 34.

- **Now I'm going to ask you to read some sentences aloud to me.**

- **Point to the number 6 in the middle of this page.**

- **Use your best reading to read sentence 6.**

Continue in the same way for sentences 7–10.

Part Four Concept Vocabulary

Assess Concept Vocabulary Use the words at the bottom of page 26 to assess the student's ability to read this unit's concept vocabulary. Have each student read the words aloud. Mark errors on your copy. Record the student's score on the Word Reading Chart on page 34.

- **Now I'm going to ask you to read some other words aloud to me.**

- **Point to the number 11 on this page.**

- **Use your best reading to read the words in row 11.**

Continue in the same way for rows 12–15.

Phonics Words

1. fossil   pencils   zigzag   pilgrim   hundred

2. reptile   costume   suppose   escape   excite

3. happens   catches   foxes   buddies   spies

4. gripped   planning   skimming   ducked   stamping

5. unbutton   replace   dislike   disconnect   inside

Phonics Sentences

6. I gave a **basket** of plants to my mom.

7. Did Jill **invite** Mike to the picnic?

8. Miss Smith has a kitten and five **puppies**.

9. Sally **hummed** a tune I like a lot.

10. I felt **unlucky** when I lost my red socks.

Concept Words

11. ethnic   culture   homesick   translated   backgrounds

12. pioneers   perspective   territory   confused   voyage

13. route   journey   views   itineraries   transportation

14. arid   frontier   carved   canyon   guide

15. eruptions   astonishing   gigantic   unbelievable   naturally

Option 2 Group Test

Use this test if you prefer to assess in a group setting. Make a copy of the test on pages 29–33 for each student. Since the Fluency and Comprehension test, which uses the passage on page 29, is to be administered individually, you will need two copies, one for the student to read and one for you to mark. Read aloud the directions in **bold**.

Part One Fluency and Comprehension

Assess Fluency Take a one-minute sample of the student's oral reading. This part of the test should be conducted with each student individually. Give the student a copy of the fluency passage "Let's Go Spelunking!" on page 29.

- **This is a test about reading.**
- **I am going to ask you to read a story aloud to me.**
- **Use your best reading as you read this story titled "Let's Go Spelunking!"**

Have the student read aloud for one minute. Note miscues on your copy. After testing, record the words correct per minute (WCPM) on the Fluency Progress Chart on page 11.

Assess Comprehension Have the student read the story quietly. If the student has difficulty with the passage, you may read it aloud.

- **Now I want you to read the story quietly to yourself.**
- **When you finish reading, you will answer some questions about what you read.**
- **Now read about spelunking.**

When the student has finished, or when you have finished reading it aloud, say

- **Now look at page 30.**
- **Answer questions 1–5.**

Part Two Phonics Words

Make sure students are on page 31.

- **Now we are going to do something different.**
- **I will read a number and a word aloud.**
- **I will say each word twice. Fill in the circle under the word I say.**

Pause after each item to allow students time to mark their answers.

1. **Fill in the circle under the word *sudden* . . . *sudden*.**
2. **Fill in the circle under the word *escape* . . . *escape*.**
3. **Fill in the circle under the word *candies* . . . *candies*.**
4. **Fill in the circle under the word *shocking* . . . *shocking*.**
5. **Fill in the circle under the word *replace* . . . *replace*.**

Record the student's score on the Word Reading Chart on page 35.

Part Three Phonics Sentences

Make sure the students are on page 32. Begin by saying

- **Now I will read a number and a sentence aloud.**
- **Follow along as I read each sentence. Then read the three words under the sentence.**
- **Find the word that best finishes the sentence.**
- **Fill in the circle next to the best word.**

Read the numbers and sentences below. Pause after each item to allow students time to mark their answers.

6. **I gave a . . . *blank* . . . of plants to my mom. Fill in the circle next to your answer.**

7. **Did Jill . . . *blank* . . . Mike to the picnic? Fill in the circle next to your answer.**

8. **Miss Smith has a kitten and five . . . *blank*. Fill in the circle next to your answer.**

9. **Sally . . . *blank* . . . a tune I like a lot. Fill in the circle next to your answer.**

10. **I felt . . . *blank* . . . when I lost my red socks. Fill in the circle next to your answer.**

Record the student's score on the Word Reading Chart on page 35.

Part Four Concept Vocabulary

Make sure the students are on page 33. Begin by saying

- **I will read a number and the definition of a word.**
- **Fill in the circle under the word that best matches the definition.**

Pause after each item to allow students time to mark their answers.

11. **Fill in the circle under the word that means "the ways of life that a particular group of people shares."**

12. **Fill in the circle under the word that means "a point of view or a way of looking at things."**

13. **Fill in the circle under the word that means "detailed plans for trips."**

14. **Fill in the circle under the word that means "a deep valley with steep walls."**

15. **Fill in the circle under the word that means "huge or enormous."**

Record the student's score on the Word Reading Chart on page 35.

Let's Go Spelunking!

Ann almost said no when her friend Kim asked   9

her to go spelunking. She was unsure what the word   19

meant. Then she learned that spelunking is exploring   27

caves. Kim and her mother were longtime cavers.   35

They loaned Ann supplies. They gave her hiking   43

boots and a hardhat with a lamp.   50

"Caving doesn't have to be scary," said Kim.   58

"You just have to think about what you're doing.   67

Don't take any risks. If you get confused, stay in one   78

area. Always be careful! We don't want to damage   87

the cave."   89

Ann was a little nervous. Then she stepped inside   98

the cave. She forgot her fear as soon as she saw the   110

great views. She gazed at rock formations. She shined   119

her light on a small stream. She tiptoed past hundreds   129

of sleeping bats. She didn't want to wake them! That   139

day Ann got a whole new perspective on caves. She   149

hoped Kim would invite her to go caving again.   158

Comprehension

Directions Answer the following questions about the passage you just read.

1. What did Ann try for the first time?

_____

_____

_____

2. What did Kim and her mother do for Ann before they went spelunking?

_____

_____

_____

3. How did Ann feel before she went into the cave? How did she feel after she went in?

_____

_____

_____

4. What kinds of things did Ann see in the cave?

_____

_____

_____

5. What "new perspective" did Ann get about caves?

_____

_____

_____

Phonics Words

1. sudden   sadden   setting
   ◯   ◯   ◯

2. estate   escape   encase
   ◯   ◯   ◯

3. candies   candy   candles
   ◯   ◯   ◯

4. shocks   shocked   shocking
   ◯   ◯   ◯

5. replace   replant   displace
   ◯   ◯   ◯

Phonics Sentences

6. I gave a _____ of plants to my mom.

- ○ bricks
- ○ basket
- ○ button

7. Did Jill _____ Mike to the picnic?

- ○ invite
- ○ inside
- ○ insist

8. Miss Smith has a kitten and five _____.

- ○ punches
- ○ pumping
- ○ puppies

9. Sally _____ a tune I like a lot.

- ○ hopped
- ○ hummed
- ○ sipped

10. I felt _____ when I lost my red socks.

- ○ retell
- ○ disloyal
- ○ unlucky

Concept Words

11. homesick   culture   translated

        ○   ○   ○

12. perspective   device   confused

        ○   ○   ○

13. journey   itineraries   transportation

        ○   ○   ○

14. frontier   cliffs   canyon

        ○   ○   ○

15. gigantic   astonishing   unbelievable

        ○   ○   ○

Word Reading Chart for Unit 1 Assessment

Administer the Individual Test or the Group Test, not both.

Test Option 1 — Individual Test				
Phonics Words Circle the items the student missed.	**Total Items**	**Items Correct**	**Reteach**	**Retest**
1. Closed Syllables with Short Vowels *fossil, pencils, zigzag, pilgrim, hundred, happens, unbutton*	7			
2. Closed Syllables with Long Vowels *reptile, costume, suppose, escape, excite, dislike, inside*	7			
3. Plurals and Inflected Endings -*s*, -*es*, -*ies*; Spelling Change: *y* to *i* *pencils, happens, catches, foxes, buddies, spies*	6			
4. Verb Endings with and without Spelling Change: Double Final Consonant *gripped, planning, skimming, ducked, stamping*	5			
5. Prefixes *un-, re-, in-, dis-* *unbutton, replace, dislike, disconnect, inside*	5			
Phonics Words Total	**30**			
Phonics Sentences	**Total Items**	**Words Correct**	**Reteach**	**Retest**
6. Closed Syllables with Short Vowels *basket*	1			
7. Closed Syllables with Long Vowels *invite*	1			
8. Plurals and Inflected Endings, Spelling Change: *y* to *i* *puppies*	1			
9. Verb Endings, Double Final Consonant *hummed*	1			
10. Prefix *un-* *unlucky*	1			
Phonics Sentences Total	**5**			
Concept Vocabulary	**Total Items**	**Words Correct**	**Reteach**	**Retest**
11. *ethnic, culture, homesick, translated, backgrounds*	5			
12. *pioneers, perspective, territory, confused, voyage*	5			
13. *route, journey, views, itineraries, transportation*	5			
14. *arid, frontier, carved, canyon, guide*	5			
15. *eruptions, astonishing, gigantic, unbelievable, naturally*	5			
Concept Vocabulary Total	**25**			

Word Reading Chart for Unit 1 Assessment

Administer the Individual Test or the Group Test, not both.

Test Option 2 — Group Test				
Phonics Words Items 1–10. Circle the items the student missed.	**Total Items**	**Items Correct**	**Reteach**	**Retest**
Closed Syllables with Short Vowels Items 1, 6	2			
Closed Syllables with Long Vowels Items 2, 7	2			
Plurals and Inflected Endings -es, -ies; Spelling Change: y to i Items 3, 8	2			
Verb Endings with and without Spelling Change: Double Final Consonant Items 4, 9	2			
Prefixes un-, re- Items 5, 10	2			
Phonics Words Total	**10**			
Concept Vocabulary **Items 11–15**	**Total Items**	**Items Correct**	**Reteach**	**Retest**
culture, perspective, itineraries, canyon, gigantic	5			
Concept Vocabulary Total	**5**			

- **RECORD SCORES** Use this chart to record scores.

- **RETEACH PHONICS SKILLS** If the student is unable to read words with particular phonics skills, then reteach the missed phonics skills.

- **PRACTICE CONCEPT VOCABULARY** If the student cannot read tested concept vocabulary, then provide additional practice.

- **RETEST** Use the same set of words or an alternate set for retesting.

Scores for Subtests: Individual/Group				
	Phonics		Concept Vocabulary	
	Ind.	Group	Ind.	Group
100%	35	10	25	5
80%	28	8	20	4
60%	21	6	15	3

© Pearson Education D

Level D—Unit 2

My Sidewalks offers two assessment options for each unit: a one-on-one Individual Test and a Group Test. Use just one of these options with your students. The Individual Test is the preferred option for use with intervention students since it will give you more precise information about their reading skills. You do not need to administer both tests.

Option 1 Individual Test

Directions This test is to be administered one-on-one to individual students. Make two copies of the test on page 38 and of the fluency passage on page 41, one for the student and one for you to mark. Read aloud the directions in **bold**.

- **This is a test about reading. In the first part, you will read a selection aloud to me.**

Part One Fluency and Comprehension

Assess Fluency Take a one-minute sample of the student's oral reading of the passage on page 41.

- **I am going to ask you to read a selection aloud to me.**

- **Use your best reading as you read this selection titled "A Whale of a Student."**

Have the student read aloud for one minute. Note miscues on your copy. After testing, record the words correct per minute (wcPM) on the Fluency Progress Chart on page 11.

Assess Comprehension Have the student read the selection quietly. If the student has difficulty with the passage, you may read it aloud.

- **Now I want you to read the selection quietly to yourself.**

- **When you finish reading, I will ask you to tell me about what you read.**

- **Now read about whales.**

When the student has finished, or when you have finished reading it aloud, ask

- **What is the selection mostly about?**

- **What is important to know about training whales?**

- **What did you learn from reading this selection?**

Use the Expository Retelling Scoring Rubric on page 13 to evaluate the student's retelling.

Part Two Phonics Words

Assess Phonics Skills Use the words at the top of page 38 to assess the student's ability to read words with this unit's phonics skills. Have each student read the words aloud. Mark errors on your copy. Record the student's score on the Word Reading Chart on page 46.

- **Now I'm going to ask you to read some words aloud to me.**

- **Point to the number 1 at the top of this page.**

- **Use your best reading to read the words in row 1.**

Continue in the same way for rows 2–5.

Part Three Phonics Sentences

Assess Phonics Skills Use the sentences in the middle of page 38 to assess the student's ability to read sentences with this unit's phonics skills. Have each student read the sentences aloud. Listen for the student's pronunciation of the phonics word in **bold** in each sentence. Mark errors on your copy. Record the student's score on the Word Reading Chart on page 46.

- **Now I'm going to ask you to read some sentences aloud to me.**

- **Point to the number 6 in the middle of this page.**

- **Use your best reading to read sentence 6.**

Continue in the same way for sentences 7–10.

Part Four Concept Vocabulary

Assess Concept Vocabulary Use the words at the bottom of page 38 to assess the student's ability to read this unit's concept vocabulary. Have each student read the words aloud. Mark errors on your copy. Record the student's score on the Word Reading Chart on page 46.

- **Now I'm going to ask you to read some other words aloud to me.**

- **Point to the number 11 on this page.**

- **Use your best reading to read the words in row 11.**

Continue in the same way for rows 12–15.

Phonics Words

1. garlic   harvest   ignore   popcorn   important

2. thirsty   circus   serpent   perfection   hamburger

3. paler   tamest   snappier   sillier   stickiest

4. camel   vivid   salad   pony   event

5. suddenly   hopeful   closeness   sadness   timeless

Phonics Sentences

6. Herman liked the **story** about the old fort.

7. James felt the stiff **whisker** of a kitten.

8. Linn's ladder is **safer** than mine.

9. It is a short bike ride to our **local** park.

10. My sister walked **slowly** along the shore.

Concept Words

11. horizons   exhibit   interactive   experience   comprehend

12. collaboration   members   accomplished   orchestra   cooperate

13. inspiration   fantastic   skillful   extraordinary   sculptures

14. career   option   contribution   energy   workers

15. capital   executive   museum   dedicated   memorabilia

Option 2 Group Test

Use this test if you prefer to assess in a group setting. Make a copy of the test on pages 41–45 for each student. Since the Fluency and Comprehension test, which uses the passage on page 41, is to be administered individually, you will need two copies, one for the student to read and one for you to mark. Read aloud the directions in **bold**.

Part One Fluency and Comprehension

Assess Fluency Take a one-minute sample of the student's oral reading. Note miscues on your copy. This part of the test should be conducted with each student individually. Give the student a copy of the fluency passage "A Whale of a Student" on page 41.

- **This is a test about reading.**
- **I am going to ask you to read a selection aloud to me.**
- **Use your best reading as you read this selection titled "A Whale of a Student."**

Have the student read aloud for one minute. Note miscues on your copy. After testing, record the words correct per minute (WCPM) on the Fluency Progress Chart on page 11.

Assess Comprehension Have the student read the selection quietly. If the student has difficulty with the passage, you may read it aloud.

- **Now I want you to read the selection quietly to yourself.**
- **When you finish reading, you will answer some questions about what you read.**
- **Now read about whales.**

When the student has finished, or when you have finished reading it aloud, say

- **Now look at page 42.**
- **Answer questions 1–5.**

Part Two Phonics Words

Make sure students are on page 43.

- **Now we are going to do something different.**
- **I will read a number and a word aloud.**
- **I will say each word twice. Fill in the circle under the word I say.**

Pause after each item to allow students time to mark their answers.

1. Fill in the circle under the word *garlic . . . garlic.*

2. Fill in the circle under the word *thirsty . . . thirsty.*

3. Fill in the circle under the word *stickiest . . . stickiest.*

4. Fill in the circle under the word *event . . . event.*

5. Fill in the circle under the word *helpful . . . helpful.*

Record the student's score on the Word Reading Chart on page 47.

Part Three Phonics Sentences

Make sure the students are on page 44. Begin by saying

- **Now I will read a number and a sentence aloud.**

- **Follow along as I read each sentence. Then read the three words under the sentence.**

- **Find the word that best finishes the sentence.**

- **Fill in the circle next to the best word.**

Read the numbers and sentences below. Pause after each item to allow students time to mark their answers.

6. **Herman liked the . . . *blank* . . . about the old fort. Fill in the circle next to your answer.**

7. **James felt the stiff . . . *blank* . . . of his kitten. Fill in the circle next to your answer.**

8. **Linn's ladder is . . . *blank* . . . than mine. Fill in the circle next to your answer.**

9. **It is a short bike ride to our . . . *blank* . . . park. Fill in the circle next to your answer.**

10. **My sister walked . . . *blank* . . . along the shore. Fill in the circle next to your answer.**

Record the student's score on the Word Reading Chart on page 43.

Part Four Concept Vocabulary

Make sure the students are on page 45. Begin by saying

- **I will read a number and the definition of a word.**

- **Fill in the circle under the word that best matches the definition.**

Pause after each item to allow students time to mark their answers.

11. **Fill in the circle under the word that means "to understand or to grasp the meaning of."**

12. **Fill in the circle under the word that means "cooperation or the act of working together with others."**

13. **Fill in the circle under the word that means "special, different, or beyond what is usual."**

14. **Fill in the circle under the word that means "the kind of job or profession a person works at."**

15. **Fill in the circle under the word that means "a place where things such as works of art or science exhibits are displayed."**

Record the student's score on the Word Reading Chart on page 47.

A Whale of a Student

It's not hard to train a small animal. To teach a   11

pup to sit, gently force it into position. Hold it in   22

place. Repeat *sit*. Then reward it with a treat. In no   33

time, you've accomplished the task. But what if you   42

want to train a huge whale to jump on command?   52

That's harder. The idea is the same, though.   60

Skillful trainers start by getting to know their   68

animal. They find out what it thinks is a treat. Would   79

you like your teacher to squirt you with water when   89

you answer a question correctly? Maybe not, but   97

some whales love the experience.   102

Once trainers know what makes their animal   109

happiest, they know how to reward it. They watch   118

and wait. When the whale jumps naturally, they   126

give the signal that means "jump." Then they give   135

the reward. Soon the whale comprehends what to do.   144

It is glad to cooperate. It may even star in a water   156

park show!   158

Comprehension

Directions Answer the following questions about the passage you just read.

1. What is the passage mostly about?

_____

_____

_____

2. How does a dog trainer teach a dog to sit?

_____

_____

_____

3. What is the first thing a whale trainer must do?

_____

_____

_____

4. How is training a whale like training smaller animals? How is it different?

_____

_____

_____

5. Why would a whale be "glad to cooperate" with its trainer?

_____

_____

Phonics Words

1. garment   garlic   gory

     ○   ○   ○

2. thirsty   thorn   Thursday

     ○   ○   ○

3. sticking   stickier   stickiest

     ○   ○   ○

4. event   ever   effect

     ○   ○   ○

5. helping   helpful   hopeless

     ○   ○   ○

Phonics Sentences

6. Herman liked the _____ about the old fort.

- ○ story
- ○ starlit
- ○ sorest

7. James felt the stiff _____ of his kitten.

- ○ whisper
- ○ whisker
- ○ wishful

8. Linn's ladder is _____ than mine.

- ○ safely
- ○ safest
- ○ safer

9. It is a short bike ride to our _____ park.

- ○ local
- ○ logic
- ○ locker

10. My sister walked _____ along the shore.

- ○ slowly
- ○ slowness
- ○ joyful

Concept Words

11. experience   exhibit   comprehend
          ○   ○   ○

12. collaboration   members   orchestra
          ○   ○   ○

13. sculptures   skillful   extraordinary
          ○   ○   ○

14. career   energy   workers
          ○   ○   ○

15. capital   museum   memorabilia
          ○   ○   ○

Student's Name _____

Word Reading Chart for Unit 2 Assessment

Administer the Individual Test or the Group Test, not both.

Test Option 1 — Individual Test				
Phonics Words Circle the items the student missed.	**Total Items**	**Items Correct**	**Reteach**	**Retest**
1. Syllables with *r*-Controlled *ar, or, ore* *garlic, harvest, ignore, popcorn, important*	5			
2. Syllables with *r*-Controlled *er, ir, ur* *thirsty, circus, serpent, perfection, hamburger*	5			
3. Endings *-er, -est;* Spelling Change: Drop e and *y* to *i* *paler, tamest, snappier, sillier, stickiest*	5			
4. Open and Closed Syllables *camel, vivid, salad, pony, event*	5			
5. Suffixes *-ly, -ful, -ness, -less* *suddenly, hopeful, closeness, sadness, timeless*	5			
Phonics Words Total	**25**			
Phonics Sentences	**Total Items**	**Words Correct**	**Reteach**	**Retest**
6. Syllables with *r*-Controlled *or* *story*	1			
7. Syllables with *r*-Controlled *er* *whisker*	1			
8. Ending *-er,* Spelling Change: Drop e *safer*	1			
9. Open Syllables *local*	1			
10. Suffix *-ly* *slowly*	1			
Phonics Sentences Total	**5**			
Concept Vocabulary	**Total Items**	**Words Correct**	**Reteach**	**Retest**
11. *horizons, exhibit, interactive, experience, comprehend*	5			
12. *collaboration, members, accomplished, orchestra, cooperate*	5			
13. *inspiration, fantastic, skillful, extraordinary, sculptures*	5			
14. *career, option, contribution, energy, workers*	5			
15. *capital, executive, museum, dedicated, memorabilia*	5			
Concept Vocabulary Total	**25**			

Word Reading Chart for Unit 2 Assessment

Administer the Individual Test or the Group Test, not both.

Test Option 2 — Group Test				
Phonics Words Items 1–10. Circle the items the student missed.	**Total Items**	**Items Correct**	**Reteach**	**Retest**
Syllables with *r*-Controlled *ar, or* Items 1, 6	2			
Syllables with *r*-Controlled *er, ir* Items 2, 7	2			
Endings *-er, -est*; Spelling Change: Drop *e* and *y* to i Items 3, 8	2			
Open Syllables Items 4, 9	2			
Suffixes *-ful, -ly* Items 5, 10	2			
Phonics Words Total	**10**			
Concept Vocabulary **Items 11–15**	**Total Items**	**Items Correct**	**Reteach**	**Retest**
comprehend, collaboration, extraordinary, career, museum	5			
Concept Vocabulary Total	**5**			

- **RECORD SCORES** Use this chart to record scores.
- **RETEACH PHONICS SKILLS** If the student is unable to read words with particular phonics skills, then reteach the missed phonics skills.
- **PRACTICE CONCEPT VOCABULARY** If the student cannot read tested concept vocabulary, then provide additional practice.
- **RETEST** Use the same set of words or an alternate set for retesting.

Scores for Subtests: Individual/Group				
	Phonics		Concept Vocabulary	
	Ind.	Group	Ind.	Group
100%	30	10	25	5
80%	24	8	20	4
60%	18	6	15	3

Level D—Unit 3

My Sidewalks offers two assessment options for each unit: a one-on-one Individual Test and a Group Test. Use just one of these options with your students. The Individual Test is the preferred option for use with intervention students since it will give you more precise information about their reading skills. You do not need to administer both tests.

Option 1 Individual Test

Directions This test is to be administered one-on-one to individual students. Make two copies of the test on page 50 and of the fluency passage on page 53, one for the student and one for you to mark. Read aloud the directions in **bold**.

- **This is a test about reading. In the first part, you will read a selection aloud to me.**

Part One Fluency and Comprehension

Assess Fluency Take a one-minute sample of the student's oral reading of the passage on page 53.

- **I am going to ask you to read a selection aloud to me.**
- **Use your best reading as you read this selection titled "Strange Lights in the Sky."**

Have the student read aloud for one minute. Note miscues on your copy. After testing, record the words correct per minute (WCPM) on the Fluency Progress Chart on page 11.

Assess Comprehension Have the student read the selection quietly. If the student has difficulty with the passage, you may read it aloud.

- **Now I want you to read the selection quietly to yourself.**
- **When you finish reading, I will ask you to tell me about what you read.**
- **Now read about the strange lights.**

When the student has finished, or when you have finished reading it aloud, ask

- **What is the selection mostly about?**
- **What is important for you to know about the Northern Lights?**
- **What did you learn from reading this selection?**

Use the Expository Retelling Scoring Rubric on page 13 to evaluate the student's retelling.

Part Two Phonics Words

Assess Phonics Skills Use the words at the top of page 50 to assess the student's ability to read words with this unit's phonics skills. Have each student read the words aloud. Mark errors on your copy. Record the student's score on the Word Reading Chart on page 58.

- **Now I'm going to ask you to read some words aloud to me.**
- **Point to the number 1 at the top of this page.**
- **Use your best reading to read the words in row 1.**

Continue in the same way for rows 2–5.

© Pearson Education D

Part Three Phonics Sentences

Assess Phonics Skills Use the sentences in the middle of page 50 to assess the student's ability to read sentences with this unit's phonics skills. Have each student read the sentences aloud. Listen for the student's pronunciation of the phonics word in **bold** in each sentence. Mark errors on your copy. Record the student's score on the Word Reading Chart on page 58.

- **Now I'm going to ask you to read some sentences aloud to me.**
- **Point to the number 6 in the middle of this page.**
- **Use your best reading to read sentence 6.**

Continue in the same way for sentences 7–10.

Part Four Concept Vocabulary

Assess Concept Vocabulary Use the words at the bottom of page 50 to assess the student's ability to read this unit's concept vocabulary. Have each student read the words aloud. Mark errors on your copy. Record the student's score on the Word Reading Chart on page 58.

- **Now I'm going to ask you to read some other words aloud to me.**
- **Point to the number 11 on this page.**
- **Use your best reading to read the words in row 11.**

Continue in the same way for rows 12–15.

Phonics Words

1. portray   Saturday   claim   dainty   complain

2. be   beehive   seeded   treason   peaceful

3. don't   won't   aren't   she'll   we've

4. oatmeal   boastful   growth   showcase   snowflake

5. mistreat   nonstop   overflow   prepaid   midseason

Phonics Sentences

6. Daisy didn't **explain** the problem to me.

7. Rain **streamed** over the rim of my hat.

8. Joan **doesn't** want to go sailing on the boat.

9. Steve **toasted** his dinner over the campfire.

10. Let's eat the grapes before they get **overripe**.

Concept Words

11. equinox   solstice   calendar   lunar   calculate

12. observe   zones   shelter   refuges   nocturnal

13. rotation   vacation   hemisphere   revolution   unpredictable

14. phenomenon   inland   tsunami   behavior   coast

15. hydrogen   solar   benefits   resources   electricity

Option 2 Group Test

Use this test if you prefer to assess in a group setting. Make a copy of the test on pages 53–57 for each student. Since the Fluency and Comprehension test, which uses the passage on page 53, is to be administered individually, you will need two copies, one for the student to read and one for you to mark. Read aloud the directions in **bold**.

Part One Fluency and Comprehension

Assess Fluency Take a one-minute sample of the student's oral reading. This part of the test should be conducted with each student individually. Give the student a copy of the fluency passage "Strange Lights in the Sky" on page 53.

- **This is a test about reading.**
- **I am going to ask you to read a selection aloud to me.**
- **Use your best reading as you read this selection titled "Strange Lights in the Sky."**

Have the student read aloud for one minute. Note miscues on your copy. After testing, record the words correct per minute (WCPM) on the Fluency Progress Chart on page 11.

Assess Comprehension Have the student read the selection quietly. If the student has difficulty with the passage, you may read it aloud.

- **Now I want you to read the selection quietly to yourself.**
- **When you finish reading, you will answer some questions about what you read.**
- **Now read about the strange lights.**

When the student has finished, or when you have finished reading it aloud, say

- **Now look at page 54.**
- **Answer questions 1–5.**

Part Two Phonics Words

Make sure students are on page 55.

- **Now we are going to do something different.**
- **I will read a number and a word aloud.**
- **I will say each word twice. Fill in the circle under the word I say.**

Pause after each item to allow students time to mark their answers.

1. Fill in the circle under the word *daily . . . daily.*

2. Fill in the circle under the word *beehive . . . beehive.*

3. Fill in the circle under the word *don't . . . don't.*

4. Fill in the circle under the word *showplace . . . showplace.*

5. Fill in the circle under the word *misspent . . . misspent.*

Record the student's score on the Word Reading Chart on page 59.

Part Three Phonics Sentences

Make sure the students are on page 56. Begin by saying

- **Now I will read a number and a sentence aloud.**

- **Follow along as I read each sentence. Then read the three words under the sentence.**

- **Find the word that best finishes the sentence.**

- **Fill in the circle next to the best word.**

Read the numbers and sentences below. Pause after each item to allow students time to mark their answers.

6. **Daisy didn't . . . *blank* . . . the problem to me. Fill in the circle next to your answer.**

7. **Rain . . . *blank* . . . over the rim of my hat. Fill in the circle next to your answer.**

8. **Joan . . . *blank* . . . want to go sailing on the boat. Fill in the circle next to your answer.**

9. **Steve . . . *blank* . . . his dinner over the campfire. Fill in the circle next to your answer.**

10. **Let's eat the grapes before they get . . . *blank*. Fill in the circle next to your answer.**

Record the student's score on the Word Reading Chart on page 59.

Part Four Concept Vocabulary

Make sure the students are on page 57. Begin by saying

- **I will read a number and the definition of a word.**

- **Fill in the circle under the word that best matches the definition.**

Pause after each item to allow students time to mark their answers.

11. **Fill in the circle under the word that means "having to do with the moon."**

12. **Fill in the circle under the word that means "places of safety or protection."**

13. **Fill in the circle under the word that means "the act of spinning or turning on an axis."**

14. **Fill in the circle under the word that means "a fact or event that can be observed."**

15. **Fill in the circle under the word that means "good things, advantages, or things that help people."**

Record the student's score on the Word Reading Chart on page 59.

Strange Lights in the Sky

People in northern cities such as Fairbanks,   7

Alaska, can often observe a stunning nocturnal sight.   15

It's the Aurora Borealis, or the Northern Lights. A   24

curtain of colors shines in the coal-black sky. The   34

colors form shapes that are constantly changing. Long   42

ago, the Northern Lights were a mystery. The people   51

of Finland told a folk tale to explain the phenomenon.   61

An arctic fox, they said, brushed his tail across the   71

snow. His bushy tail started fires. It also scattered   80

snow into the air. The Northern Lights were the   89

reflection of the fires in the snow.   96

We can still enjoy folk tales. But we have a   106

scientific explanation as well. The sun gives off   114

gases. The gases leave the sun in the form of the solar   126

wind. The solar wind travels toward Earth for about   135

three days. Then it crashes into Earth's magnetic   143

field. When the two forces clash, electricity is created.   152

This causes a glow. The glow lights the midnight sky.   162

Comprehension

Directions Answer the following questions about the passage you just read.

1. What can people who live in the far north sometimes see in the night sky?

   _____

   _____

2. How are the Northern Lights different from city street lights?

   _____

   _____

3. How did people in Finland explain the Northern Lights before they knew of a scientific explanation?

   _____

   _____

4. What is the explanation of the Northern Lights today?

   _____

   _____

5. Which explanation of the Northern Lights is more useful to scientists, the tale about a fox or the details about the sun, Earth, and electricity?

   _____

   _____

Phonics Words

1. darkness   daily   dandy

○   ○   ○

2. bench   beehive   bending

○   ○   ○

3. don't   dent   didn't

○   ○   ○

4. seashore   shower   showplace

○   ○   ○

5. misspent   mister   misty

○   ○   ○

Phonics Sentences

6. Daisy didn't _____ the problem to me.

- ○ restrain
- ○ explain
- ○ mislay

7. Rain _____ over the rim of my hat.

- ○ streamed
- ○ steered
- ○ screamed

8. Joan _____ want to go sailing on the boat.

- ○ isn't
- ○ aren't
- ○ doesn't

9. Steve _____ his dinner over the campfire.

- ○ coaster
- ○ flow
- ○ toasted

10. Let's eat the grapes before they get _____.

- ○ overripe
- ○ overeat
- ○ midyear

Concept Words

11.   solar   lunar   calculate

     ○   ○   ○

12.   observe   solstice   refuges

     ○   ○   ○

13.   rotation   hemisphere   unpredictable

     ○   ○   ○

14.   phenomenon   hydrogen   warning

     ○   ○   ○

15.   benefits   resources   electricity

     ○   ○   ○

Word Reading Chart for Unit 3 Assessment

Administer the Individual Test or the Group Test, not both.

Test Option 1 — Individual Test				
Phonics Words Circle the items the student missed.	**Total Items**	**Items Correct**	**Reteach**	**Retest**
1. Syllables with Long *a* Spelled *ai, ay* portray, Saturday, claim, dainty, complain, prepaid	6			
2. Syllables with Long *e* Spelled *e, ee, ea* be, beehive, seeded, treason, peaceful, oatmeal, mistreat, midseason	8			
3. Contractions *don't, won't, aren't, she'll, we've*	5			
4. Syllables with Long *o* Spelled *oa, ow* oatmeal, boastful, growth, showcase, snowflake, overflow	6			
5. Prefixes *mis-, non-, over-, pre-, mid-* mistreat, nonstop, overflow, prepaid, midseason	5			
Phonics Words Total	**30**			
Phonics Sentences	**Total Items**	**Words Correct**	**Reteach**	**Retest**
6. Syllables with Long *a* Spelled *ai* explain	1			
7. Syllables with Long *e* Spelled *ea* streamed	1			
8. Contractions *doesn't*	1			
9. Syllables with Long *o* Spelled *oa* toasted	1			
10. Prefix *over-* overripe	1			
Phonics Sentences Total	**5**			
Concept Vocabulary	**Total Items**	**Words Correct**	**Reteach**	**Retest**
11. *equinox, solstice, calendar, lunar, calculate*	5			
12. *observe, zones, shelter, refuges, nocturnal*	5			
13. *rotation, vacation, hemisphere, revolution, unpredictable*	5			
14. *phenomenon, inland, tsunami, behavior, coast*	5			
15. *hydrogen, solar, benefits, resources, electricity*	5			
Concept Vocabulary Total	**25**			

Word Reading Chart for Unit 3 Assessment

Administer the Individual Test or the Group Test, not both.

Test Option 2 — Group Test				
Phonics Words Items 1–10. Circle the items the student missed.	**Total Items**	**Items Correct**	**Reteach**	**Retest**
Syllables with Long *a* Spelled *ai, ay* Items 1, 6	2			
Syllables with Long *e* Spelled *ee, ea* Items 2, 7	2			
Contractions Items 3, 8	2			
Syllables with Long *o* Spelled *oa, ow* Items 4, 9	2			
Prefixes *mis-, over-* Items 5, 10	2			
Phonics Words Total	**10**			
Concept Vocabulary **Items 11–15**	**Total Items**	**Items Correct**	**Reteach**	**Retest**
lunar, refuges, rotation, phenomenon, benefits	5			
Concept Vocabulary Total	**5**			

- **RECORD SCORES** Use this chart to record scores.
- **RETEACH PHONICS SKILLS** If the student is unable to read words with particular phonics skills, then reteach the missed phonics skills.
- **PRACTICE CONCEPT VOCABULARY** If the student cannot read tested concept vocabulary, then provide additional practice.
- **RETEST** Use the same set of words or an alternate set for retesting.

Scores for Subtests: Individual/Group				
	Phonics		Concept Vocabulary	
	Ind.	Group	Ind.	Group
100%	35	10	25	5
80%	28	8	20	4
60%	21	6	15	3

Level D—Unit 4

My Sidewalks offers two assessment options for each unit: a one-on-one Individual Test and a Group Test. Use just one of these options with your students. The Individual Test is the preferred option for use with intervention students since it will give you more precise information about their reading skills. You do not need to administer both tests.

Option 1 Individual Test

Directions This test is to be administered one-on-one to individual students. Make two copies of the test on page 62 and of the fluency passage on page 65, one for the student and one for you to mark. Read aloud the directions in **bold**.

- **This is a test about reading. In the first part, you will read a selection aloud to me.**

Part One Fluency and Comprehension

Assess Fluency Take a one-minute sample of the student's oral reading of the passage on page 65.

- **I am going to ask you to read a selection aloud to me.**

- **Use your best reading as you read this selection titled "Houdini, Master of Illusions."**

Have the student read aloud for one minute. Note miscues on your copy. After testing, record the words correct per minute (WCPM) on the Fluency Progress Chart on page 11.

Assess Comprehension Have the student read the selection quietly. If the student has difficulty with the passage, you may read it aloud.

- **Now I want you to read the selection quietly to yourself.**

- **When you finish reading, I will ask you to tell me about what you read.**

- **Now read about Harry Houdini.**

When the student has finished, or when you have finished reading it aloud, ask

- **What is the selection mostly about?**

- **What is important for you to know about Harry Houdini?**

- **What did you learn from reading this selection?**

Use the Expository Retelling Scoring Rubric on page 13 to evaluate the student's retelling.

Part Two Phonics Words

Assess Phonics Skills Use the words at the top of page 62 to assess the student's ability to read words with this unit's phonics skills. Have each student read the words aloud. Record the student's score on the Word Reading Chart on page 70.

- **Now I'm going to ask you to read some words aloud to me.**

- **Point to the number 1 at the top of this page.**

- **Use your best reading to read the words in row 1.**

Continue in the same way for rows 2–5.

© Pearson Education D

Part Three Phonics Sentences

Assess Phonics Skills Use the sentences in the middle of page 62 to assess the student's ability to read sentences with this unit's phonics skills. Have each student read the sentences aloud. Listen for the student's pronunciation of the phonics word in **bold** in each sentence. Mark errors on your copy. Record the student's score on the Word Reading Chart on page 70.

- **Now I'm going to ask you to read some sentences aloud to me.**
- **Point to the number 6 in the middle of this page.**
- **Use your best reading to read sentence 6.**

Continue in the same way for sentences 7–10.

Part Four Concept Vocabulary

Assess Concept Vocabulary Use the words at the bottom of page 62 to assess the student's ability to read this unit's concept vocabulary. Have each student read the words aloud. Mark errors on your copy. Record the student's score on the Word Reading Chart on page 70.

- **Now I'm going to ask you to read some other words aloud to me.**
- **Point to the number 11 on this page.**
- **Use your best reading to read the words in row 11.**

Continue in the same way for rows 12–15.

Phonics Words

1. rattlesnake   handcuffs   tabletop   cannot   yardstick

2. high   might   lie   flying   why

3. chuckle   handle   purple   bundle   jumble

4. shouts   counter   south   thousands   how

5. glamorous   diver   explorer   joyous   actor

Phonics Sentences

6. We **cannot** go outside today because it is raining too hard.

7. The eagle soared **high** in the sky.

8. The belt had a big gold **buckle**.

9. A **loud** noise scared the sleeping dog.

10. The brave **explorer** reached the top of the mountain.

Concept Words

11. invisible   illusion   perception   vanish   magician

12. instinct   response   sense   young   protect

13. creative   discovered   treasure   solution   solve

14. conversation   symbols   dialect   combine   region

15. scrutiny   evidence   convince   diver   explorer

Option 2 Group Test

Use this test if you prefer to assess in a group setting. Make a copy of the test on pages 65–69 for each student. Since the Fluency and Comprehension test, which uses the passage on page 61, is to be administered individually, you will need two copies, one for the student to read and one for you to mark. Read aloud the directions in **bold**.

Part One Fluency and Comprehension

Assess Fluency Take a one-minute sample of the student's oral reading. Note miscues on your copy. This part of the test should be conducted with each student individually. Give the student a copy of the fluency passage "Houdini, Master of Illusions" on page 65.

- **This is a test about reading.**
- **I am going to ask you to read a selection aloud to me.**
- **Use your best reading as you read this selection titled "Houdini, Master of Illusions."**

Have the student read aloud for one minute. Note miscues on your copy. After testing, record the words correct per minute (wcpm) on the Fluency Progress Chart on page 11.

Assess Comprehension Have the student read the selection quietly. If the student has difficulty with the passage, you may read it aloud.

- **Now I want you to read the selection quietly to yourself.**
- **When you finish reading, you will answer some questions about what you read.**
- **Now read about Harry Houdini.**

When the student has finished, or when you have finished reading it aloud, say

- **Now look at page 66.**
- **Answer questions 1–5.**

Part Two Phonics Words

Make sure students are on page 67.

- **Now we are going to do something different.**
- **I will read a number and a word aloud.**
- **I will say each word twice. Fill in the circle under the word I say.**

Pause after each item to allow students time to mark their answers.

1. **Fill in the circle under the word *underground* . . . *underground*.**
2. **Fill in the circle under the word *might* . . . *might*.**
3. **Fill in the circle under the word *handle* . . . *handle*.**
4. **Fill in the circle under the word *south* . . . *south*.**
5. **Fill in the circle under the word *glamorous* . . . *glamorous*.**

Record the student's score on the Word Reading Chart on page 71.

Part Three Phonics Sentences

Make sure the students are on page 68. Begin by saying

- **Now I will read a number and a sentence aloud.**

- **Follow along as I read each sentence. Then read the three words under the sentence.**

- **Find the word that best finishes the sentence.**

- **Fill in the circle next to the best word.**

- **Read the completed sentence aloud to me.**

Read the numbers and sentences below. Pause after each item to allow students time to mark their answers.

6. **We** . . . *blank* . . . **go outside today because it is raining too hard. Fill in the circle next to your answer.**

7. **The eagle soared** . . . *blank* . . . **in the sky. Fill in the circle next to your answer.**

8. **The belt had a big gold** . . . *blank.* **Fill in the circle next to your answer.**

9. **A** . . . *blank* . . . **noise scared the sleeping dog. Fill in the circle next to your answer.**

10. **The brave** . . . *blank* . . . **reached the top of the mountain. Fill in the circle next to your answer.**

Record the student's score on the Word Reading Chart on page 71.

Part Four Concept Vocabulary

Make sure the students are on page 69. Begin by saying

- **I will read a number and the definition of a word.**

- **Fill in the circle under the word that best matches the definition.**

Pause after each item to allow students time to mark their answers.

11. **Fill in the circle under the word that means "to disappear, especially suddenly."**

12. **Fill in the circle under the word that means "a reaction by a living thing."**

13. **Fill in the circle under the word that means "an explanation or the solving of a problem."**

14. **Fill in the circle under the word that means "a form of a language spoken by a certain group of people."**

15. **Fill in the circle under the word that means "facts, proof, or anything that shows or makes clear."**

Record the student's score on the Word Reading Chart on page 71.

Houdini, Master of Illusions

Harry Houdini was a great magician. He became famous 9

around the world. Handcuffs and prison cells could not hold 19

him. He escaped from locked boxes full of water. He could make 31

an elephant disappear. 34

How did he do it? Some of it was hard work and skill. But 48

Houdini was also good at fooling people. Did the elephant really 59

vanish? No, it was an illusion. 65

Houdini was good at creating illusions. An illusion is 74

something that seems to happen but really can't. If a table 85

seemed to float through the air, that was an illusion. Tables 96

can't float. If a rabbit appeared in an empty hat, it was an 109

illusion. Rabbits can't appear out of thin air. And a disappearing 120

elephant? You guessed it—it was an illusion. Houdini's tricks 130

fooled people. They thought they saw an elephant vanish. It 140

didn't really happen. 143

Comprehension

Directions Answer the following questions about the passage you just read.

1. What do you think is important to understand about Harry Houdini?

_____

_____

_____

2. Why is a table floating through the air an illusion?

_____

_____

_____

3. What other illusions could Houdini perform?

_____

_____

_____

4. Why might Harry Houdini be called a "master of illusions"?

_____

_____

_____

5. How are having a rabbit appear in a hat and having an elephant disappear alike? How are these tricks different?

_____

_____

_____

Phonics Words

1. underground   groundhog   underneath
   ○   ○   ○

2. mint   might   mine
   ○   ○   ○

3. handful   hardly   handle
   ○   ○   ○

4. south   soothe   shout
   ○   ○   ○

5. glancing   glassmaker   glamorous
   ○   ○   ○

Phonics Sentences

6. We _____ go outside today because it is raining too hard.

   ○ cannot

   ○ anything

   ○ afternoon

7. The eagle soared _____ in the sky.

   ○ rough

   ○ high

   ○ fly

8. The belt had a big gold _____.

   ○ bubble

   ○ bumble

   ○ buckle

9. A _____ noise scared the sleeping dog.

   ○ shouts

   ○ loud

   ○ how

10. The brave _____ reached the top of the mountain.

   ○ diver

   ○ joyous

   ○ explorer

Concept Words

11.   vanish   mysterious   perception

        ○   ○   ○

12.   young   response   protect

        ○   ○   ○

13.   creative   treasure   solution

        ○   ○   ○

14.   symbols   dialect   combine

        ○   ○   ○

15.   evidence   curious   explorer

        ○   ○   ○

Word Reading Chart for Unit 4 Assessment

Administer the Individual Test or the Group Test, not both.

Test Option 1 — Individual Test				
Phonics Words Circle the items the student missed.	**Total Items**	**Items Correct**	**Reteach**	**Retest**
1. Compound Words *rattlesnake, handcuffs, tabletop, cannot, yardstick*	5			
2. Long *i* Spelled *igh, ie,* final *y* *high, might, lie, flying, why*	5			
3. Consonant + *le* Syllables *chuckle, handle, purple, bundle, jumble*	5			
4. Diphthongs *ou, ow/ou/* *shouts, counter, south, thousands, how*	5			
5. Suffixes *-er, -or, -ous* *glamorous, diver, explorer, joyous, actor*	5			
Phonics Words Total	**25**			
Phonics Sentences	**Total Items**	**Words Correct**	**Reteach**	**Retest**
6. Compound Words *cannot*	1			
7. Long *i* Spelled *igh* *high*	1			
8. Consonant + *le* Syllables *buckle*	1			
9. Diphthong *ou* *loud*	1			
10. Suffix *-er* *explorer*	1			
Phonics Sentences Total	**5**			
Concept Vocabulary	**Total Items**	**Words Correct**	**Reteach**	**Retest**
11. *invisible, illusion, perception, vanish, magician*	5			
12. *instinct, response, sense, young, protect*	5			
13. *creative, discovered, treasure, solution, solve*	5			
14. *conversation, symbols, dialect, combine, region*	5			
15. *scrutiny, evidence, convince, diver, explorer*	5			
Concept Vocabulary Total	**25**			

Word Reading Chart for Unit 4 Assessment

Administer the Individual Test or the Group Test, not both.

Test Option 2 — Group Test				
Phonics Words Items 1–10. Circle the items the student missed.	**Total Items**	**Items Correct**	**Reteach**	**Retest**
Compound Words Items 1, 6	2			
Long *i* Spelled *igh* Items 2, 7	2			
Consonants + *le* Syllables Items 3, 8	2			
Diphthong *ou* Items 4, 9	2			
Suffixes *-er, -ous* Items 5, 10	2			
Phonics Words Total	**10**			
Concept Vocabulary **Items 11–15**	**Total Items**	**Items Correct**	**Reteach**	**Retest**
vanish, response, solution, dialect, evidence	5			
Concept Vocabulary Total	**5**			

- **RECORD SCORES** Use this chart to record scores.
- **RETEACH PHONICS SKILLS** If the student is unable to read words with particular phonics skills, then reteach the missed phonics skills.
- **PRACTICE CONCEPT VOCABULARY** If the student cannot read tested concept vocabulary, then provide additional practice.
- **RETEST** Use the same set of words or an alternate set for retesting.

Scores for Subtests: Individual/Group				
	Phonics		Concept Vocabulary	
	Ind.	Group	Ind.	Group
100%	30	10	25	5
80%	24	8	20	4
60%	18	6	15	3

Level D—Unit 5

My Sidewalks offers two assessment options for each unit: a one-on-one Individual Test and a Group Test. Use just one of these options with your students. The Individual Test is the preferred option for use with intervention students since it will give you more precise information about their reading skills. You do not need to administer both tests.

Option 1 Individual Test

Directions This test is to be administered one-on-one to individual students. Make two copies of the test on page 74 and of the fluency passage on page 77, one for the student and one for you to mark. Read aloud the directions in **bold**.

- **This is a test about reading. In the first part, you will read a story aloud to me.**

Part One Fluency and Comprehension

Assess Fluency Take a one-minute sample of the student's oral reading of the passage on page 77.

- **I am going to ask you to read a story aloud to me.**

- **Use your best reading as you read this story titled "*Alvin,* the Explorer."**

Have the student read aloud for one minute. Note miscues on your copy. After testing, record the words correct per minute (wcpm) on the Fluency Progress Chart on page 11.

Assess Comprehension Have the student read the selection quietly. If the student has difficulty with the passage, you may read it aloud.

- **Now I want you to read the story quietly to yourself.**

- **When you finish reading, I will ask you to tell me about what you read.**

- **Now read about *Alvin*.**

When the student has finished, or when you have finished reading it aloud, ask

- **Who is this story about?**

- **Where or when does this story take place?**

- **What is the problem or goal? How is the problem solved or the goal achieved?**

Use the Narrative Retelling Scoring Rubric on page 12 to evaluate the student's retelling.

Part Two Phonics Words

Assess Phonics Skills Use the words at the top of page 74 to assess the student's ability to read words with this unit's phonics skills. Have each student read the words aloud. Mark errors on your copy. Record the student's score on the Word Reading Chart on page 82.

- **Now I'm going to ask you to read some words aloud to me.**

- **Point to the number 1 at the top of this page.**

- **Use your best reading to read the words in row 1.**

Continue in the same way for rows 2–5.

Part Three Phonics Sentences

Assess Phonics Skills Use the sentences in the middle of page 74 to assess the student's ability to read sentences with this unit's phonics skills. Have each student read the sentences aloud. Listen for the student's pronunciation of the phonics word in **bold** in each sentence. Mark errors on your copy. Record the student's score on the Word Reading Chart on page 82.

- **Now I'm going to ask you to read some sentences aloud to me.**
- **Point to the number 6 in the middle of this page.**
- **Use your best reading to read sentence 6.**

Continue in the same way for sentences 7–10.

Part Four Concept Vocabulary

Assess Concept Vocabulary Use the words at the bottom of page 74 to assess the student's ability to read this unit's concept vocabulary. Have each student read the words aloud. Mark errors on your copy. Record the student's score on the Word Reading Chart on page 82.

- **Now I'm going to ask you to read some other words aloud to me.**
- **Point to the number 11 on this page.**
- **Use your best reading to read the words in row 11.**

Continue in the same way for rows 12–15.

Phonics Words

1. moist   broil   poison   joyful   toyshop

2. union   mention   station   vision   picture

3. moose   scooter   threw   jewel   value

4. sidewalk   always   August   sprawl   slaughter

5. girlhood   statement   ashen   creaky   stormy

Phonics Sentences

6. Joy hoped the noise would not **annoy** her classmates.

7. The class **discussion** helped Roy understand the lesson.

8. Jenny saw a dentist when she lost a **tooth**.

9. My sister's **cough** woke me up every hour.

10. We stared in **amazement** at the heap of silver coins.

Concept Words

11. aquarium   isolated   oxygen   artifacts   destroyed

12. civilization   society   ancient   statue   traditions

13. dangerous   profession   expeditions   wilderness   adventure

14. adapted   burrow   extreme   prairie   homesteaders

15. craters   satellite   myths   mission   astronaut

Option 2 Group Test

Use this test if you prefer to assess in a group setting. Make a copy of the test on pages 77–81 for each student. Since the Fluency and Comprehension test, which uses the passage on page 77, is to be administered individually, you will need two copies, one for the student to read and one for you to mark. Read aloud the directions in **bold**.

Part One Fluency and Comprehension

Assess Fluency Take a one-minute sample of the student's oral reading. This part of the test should be conducted with each student individually. Give the student a copy of the fluency passage "*Alvin,* the Explorer" on page 77.

- **This is a test about reading.**
- **I am going to ask you to read a story aloud to me.**
- **Use your best reading as you read this story titled "*Alvin,* the Explorer."**

Have the student read aloud for one minute. Note miscues on your copy. After testing, record the words correct per minute (wcpm) on the Fluency Progress Chart on page 11.

Assess Comprehension Have the student read the story quietly. If the student has difficulty with the passage, you may read it aloud.

- **Now I want you to read the story quietly to yourself.**
- **When you finish reading, you will answer some questions about what you read.**
- **Now read about *Alvin*.**

When the student has finished, or when you have finished reading it aloud, say

- **Now look at page 78.**
- **Answer questions 1–5.**

Part Two Phonics Words

Make sure students are on page 79.

- **Now we are going to do something different.**
- **I will read a number and a word aloud.**
- **I will say each word twice. Fill in the circle under the word I say.**

Pause after each item to allow students time to mark their answers.

- **1. Fill in the circle under the word *boil* . . . *boil*.**
- **2. Fill in the circle under the word *potion* . . . *potion*.**
- **3. Fill in the circle under the word *crew* . . . *crew*.**
- **4. Fill in the circle under the word *sprawl* . . . *sprawl*.**
- **5. Fill in the circle under the word *creamy* . . . *creamy*.**

Record the student's score on the Word Reading Chart on page 83.

Part Three Phonics Sentences

Make sure the students are on page 80. Begin by saying

- **Now I will read a number and a sentence aloud.**

- **Follow along as I read each sentence. Then read the three words under the sentence.**

- **Find the word that best finishes the sentence.**

- **Fill in the circle next to the best word.**

Read the numbers and sentences below. Pause after each item to allow students time to mark their answers.

6. **Joy hoped the noise would not . . . *blank* . . . her classmates. Fill in the circle next to your answer.**

7. **The class . . . *blank* . . . helped Roy understand the lesson. Fill in the circle next to your answer.**

8. **Jenny saw a dentist when she lost a . . . *blank*. Fill in the circle next to your answer.**

9. **My sister's . . . *blank* . . . woke me up every hour. Fill in the circle next to your answer.**

10. **We stared in . . . *blank* . . . at the heap of silver coins. Fill in the circle next to your answer.**

Record the student's score on the Word Reading Chart on page 83.

Part Four Concept Vocabulary

Make sure the students are on page 81. Begin by saying

- **I will read a number and the definition of a word.**

- **Fill in the circle under the word that best matches the definition.**

Pause after each item to allow students time to mark their answers.

11. **Fill in the circle under the word that means "a tank in which fish are kept or a building that houses many tanks of fish."**

12. **Fill in the circle under the word that means "a carved or molded work of art."**

13. **Fill in the circle under the word that means "trips made for specific purposes."**

14. **Fill in the circle under the word that means "changed or adjusted to fit into certain conditions or surroundings."**

15. **Fill in the circle under the word that means" a person who travels to outer space."**

Record the student's score on the Word Reading Chart on page 83.

Name _____

Alvin, the Explorer

Two crew members climbed into the   6

submersible craft called *Alvin* and prepared for an   14

underwater expedition. They checked the oxygen   20

and moved *Alvin*'s robot arms. They adjusted the   28

camera equipment. Then they headed for their   35

destination, the extreme depths of the ocean that   43

only a submersible like *Alvin* could reach.   50

As *Alvin* descended, the blue water turned   57

black. The crew turned on the lights and began   66

taking pictures. Suddenly, the craft rocked. The crew   74

peered out the windows and saw an awful sight.   83

Alvin had been attacked by a dangerous swordfish!   91

The sword was stuck in *Alvin*'s skin, and the   100

swordfish was trapped. *Alvin* was quickly hoisted to   108

the surface. The crew checked *Alvin* carefully. Was   116

Alvin destroyed? No. *Alvin* survived with only   123

minor damage. The fish wasn't as lucky. It   131

became food for *Alvin*'s hungry crew.   137

© Pearson Education D

Comprehension

Directions Answer the following questions about the passage you just read.

1. Who or what was *Alvin?*

_____

_____

2. What equipment and supplies did *Alvin* carry?

_____

_____

3. What was the first thing the crew did after they felt the craft rock?

_____

_____

4. How did the swordfish attack affect *Alvin?* How did it affect the swordfish?

_____

_____

5. What would have happened to the crew if *Alvin* had been destroyed? Why do you think so?

_____

_____

Phonics Words

1.   bring   boil   boat
      ○   ○   ○

2.   potion   person   pointing
      ○   ○   ○

3.   crawl   crew   crept
      ○   ○   ○

4.   sprawl   spring   spread
      ○   ○   ○

5.   creamed   creation   creamy
      ○   ○   ○

Phonics Sentences

6. Joy hoped the noise would not _____ her classmates.

○ enjoy

○ annoy

○ voice

7. The class _____ helped Roy understand the lesson.

○ discussion

○ nation

○ furniture

8. Jenny saw a dentist when she lost a _____.

○ tool

○ tooth

○ true

9. My sister's _____ woke me up every hour.

○ taught

○ cough

○ caught

10. We stared in _____ at the heap of silver coins.

○ amazement

○ argument

○ falsehood

© Pearson Education D

Concept Words

11.   aquarium   isolated   artifacts

         ○   ○   ○

12.   ancient   statue   society

         ○   ○   ○

13.   expeditions   profession   wilderness

         ○   ○   ○

14.   burrow   adapted   extreme

         ○   ○   ○

15.   myths   mission   astronaut

         ○   ○   ○

Word Reading Chart for Unit 5 Assessment

Administer the Individual Test or the Group Test, not both.

Test Option 1 — Individual Test				
Phonics Words Circle the items the student missed.	**Total Items**	**Items Correct**	**Reteach**	**Retest**
1. Syllables with Diphthongs *oi, oy* *moist, broil, poison, joyful, toyshop*	5			
2. Common Syllables *ion, tion, sion, ture* *union, mention, station, vision, picture*	5			

3. Syllables with Vowel Combinations *oo, ew, ue* as in *moon,*
   flew, blue
   moose, scooter, threw, jewel, value
	5			

4. Syllables with Vowel Sound in *ball: a, al, au, aw, augh* *sidewalk, always, August, sprawl, slaughter*	5			
5. Suffixes *-hood, -ment, -y, -en* *girlhood, statement, ashen, creaky, stormy*	5			
Phonics Words Total	**25**			
Phonics Sentences	**Total Items**	**Words Correct**	**Reteach**	**Retest**
6. Syllables with Diphthong *oy* *annoy*	1			
7. Common Syllable *sion* *discussion*	1			
8. Syllables with *oo* in *moon* *tooth*	1			
9. Syllables with Vowel Sound in *ball: ough* *cough*	1			
10. Suffixes *-ment* *amazement*	1			
Phonics Sentences Total	**5**			
Concept Vocabulary	**Total Items**	**Words Correct**	**Reteach**	**Retest**
11. *aquarium, isolated, oxygen, artifacts, destroyed*	5			
12. *civilization, society, ancient, statue, traditions*	5			
13. *dangerous, profession, expeditions, wilderness, adventure*	5			
14. *adapted, burrow, extreme, prairie, homesteaders*	5			
15. *craters, satellite, myths, mission, astronaut*	5			
Concept Vocabulary Total	**25**			

Word Reading Chart for Unit 5 Assessment

Administer the Individual Test or the Group Test, not both.

Test Option 2 — Group Test				
Phonics Words Items 1–10. Circle the items the student missed.	**Total Items**	**Items Correct**	**Reteach**	**Retest**
Syllables with Diphthongs *oi, oy* Items 1, 6	2			
Common Syllables *tion, sion* Items 2, 7	2			
Syllables with *oo, ew* in *moon, flew* Items 3, 8	2			
Syllables with Vowel Sound in *ball: aw, ough* Items 4, 9	2			
Suffixes *-ment, -y* Items 5, 10	2			
Phonics Words Total	**10**			
Concept Vocabulary **Items 11–15**	**Total Items**	**Items Correct**	**Reteach**	**Retest**
aquarium, statue, expeditions, adapted, astronaut	5			
Concept Vocabulary Total	**5**			

- **RECORD SCORES** Use this chart to record scores.
- **RETEACH PHONICS SKILLS** If the student is unable to read words with particular phonics skills, then reteach the missed phonics skills.
- **PRACTICE CONCEPT VOCABULARY** If the student cannot read tested concept vocabulary, then provide additional practice.
- **RETEST** Use the same set of words or an alternate set for retesting.

Scores for Subtests: Individual/Group				
	Phonics		Concept Vocabulary	
	Ind.	Group	Ind.	Group
100%	30	10	25	5
80%	24	8	20	4
60%	18	6	15	3

Level D—Unit 6

My Sidewalks offers two assessment options for each unit: a one-on-one Individual Test and a Group Test. Use just one of these options with your students. The Individual Test is the preferred option for use with intervention students since it will give you more precise information about their reading skills. You do not need to administer both tests.

Option 1 Individual Test

Directions This test is to be administered one-on-one to individual students. Make two copies of the test on page 86 and of the fluency passage on page 89, one for the student and one for you to mark. Read aloud the directions in **bold**.

- **This is a test about reading. In the first part, you will read a story aloud to me.**

Part One Fluency and Comprehension

Assess Fluency Take a one-minute sample of the student's oral reading of the passage on page 89.

- **I am going to ask you to read a story aloud to me.**
- **Use your best reading as you read this story titled "Creative Caleb."**

Have the student read aloud for one minute. Note miscues on your copy. After testing, record the words correct per minute (WCPM) on the Fluency Progress Chart on page 11.

Assess Comprehension Have the student read the selection quietly. If the student has difficulty with the passage, you may read it aloud.

- **Now I want you to read the story quietly to yourself.**
- **When you finish reading, I will ask you to tell me about what you read.**
- **Now read about Caleb.**

When the student has finished, or when you have finished reading it aloud, ask

- **Who is this story about? Tell me more about Caleb.**
- **Where or when does the story take place?**
- **What is the problem or goal? How is the problem solved or the goal reached?**

Use the Narrative Retelling Scoring Rubric on page 12 to evaluate the student's retelling.

Part Two Phonics Words

Assess Phonics Skills Use the words at the top of page 86 to assess the student's ability to read words with this unit's phonics skills. Have each student read the words aloud. Mark errors on your copy. Record the student's score on the Word Reading Chart on page 94.

- **Now I'm going to ask you to read some words aloud to me.**
- **Point to the number 1 at the top of this page.**
- **Use your best reading to read the words in row 1.**

Continue in the same way for rows 2–5.

Part Three Phonics Sentences

Assess Phonics Skills Use the sentences in the middle of page 86 to assess the student's ability to read sentences with this unit's phonics skills. Have each student read the sentences aloud. Listen for the student's pronunciation of the phonics word in **bold** in each sentence. Mark errors on your copy. Record the student's score on the Word Reading Chart on page 94.

- **Now I'm going to ask you to read some sentences aloud to me.**
- **Point to the number 6 in the middle of this page.**
- **Use your best reading to read sentence 6.**

Continue in the same way for sentences 7–10.

Part Four Concept Vocabulary

Assess Concept Vocabulary Use the words at the bottom of page 86 to assess the student's ability to read this unit's concept vocabulary. Have each student read the words aloud. Mark errors on your copy. Record the student's score on the Word Reading Chart on page 94.

- **Now I'm going to ask you to read some other words aloud to me.**
- **Point to the number 11 on this page.**
- **Use your best reading to read the words in row 11.**

Continue in the same way for rows 12–15.

Phonics Words

1. thread   health   feather   instead   sweatshirt

2. crook   nook   cookbook   bush   cushion

3. unkind   mildly   older   scold   poster

4. create   liar   poem   radio   variety

5. relate   relative   relationship   press   pressure

Phonics Sentences

6. Let's **spread** the picnic blanket here.

7. Todd **pushed** aside his feelings of worry and stood up to bat.

8. Heather helped me **find** some of my lost books.

9. My sister played her **violin** in music class.

10. Rob is **inventive**. He invents so many clever things.

Concept Words

11. circumstances   conviction   model   procrastinates   devised

12. hurdles   perseverance   achieved   furious   personality

13. immigration   barrier   occupations   awkward   appreciate

14. atmosphere   propulsion   supersonic   efficient   gauges

15. telescope   galaxy   universe   futuristic   scientific

Option 2 Group Test

Use this test if you prefer to assess in a group setting. Make a copy of the test on pages 89–93 for each student. Since the Fluency and Comprehension test, which uses the passage on page 89, is to be administered individually, you will need two copies, one for the student to read and one for you to mark. Read aloud the directions in **bold**.

Part One Fluency and Comprehension

Assess Fluency Take a one-minute sample of the student's oral reading. This part of the test should be conducted with each student individually. Give the student a copy of the fluency passage "Creative Caleb" on page 89.

- **This is a test about reading.**
- **I am going to ask you to read a story aloud to me.**
- **Use your best reading as you read this story titled "Creative Caleb."**

Have the student read aloud for one minute. Note miscues on your copy. After testing, record the words correct per minute (WCPM) on the Fluency Progress Chart on page 11.

Assess Comprehension Have the student read the story quietly. If the student has difficulty with the passage, you may read it aloud.

- **Now I want you to read the story quietly to yourself.**
- **When you finish reading, you will answer some questions about what you read.**
- **Now read about Caleb.**

When the student has finished, or when you have finished reading it aloud, say

- **Now look at page 90.**
- **Answer questions 1–5.**

Part Two Phonics Words

Make sure students are on page 91.

- **Now we are going to do something different.**
- **I will read a number and a word aloud.**
- **I will say each word twice. Fill in the circle under the word I say.**

Pause after each item to allow students time to mark their answers.

1. **Fill in the circle under the word *dread* . . . *dread.***
2. **Fill in the circle under the word *understood* . . . *understood.***
3. **Fill in the circle under the word *scold* . . . *scold.***
4. **Fill in the circle under the word *diet* . . . *diet.***
5. **Fill in the circle under the word that is related to *create* . . . *create.***

Record the student's score on the Word Reading Chart on page 95.

Part Three Phonics Sentences

Make sure the students are on page 92. Begin by saying

- **Now I will read a number and a sentence aloud.**

- **Follow along as I read each sentence. Then read the three words under the sentence.**

- **Find the word that best finishes the sentence.**

- **Fill in the circle next to the best word.**

Read the numbers and sentences below. Pause after each item to allow students time to mark their answers.

6. **Let's . . . *blank* . . . the picnic blanket here. Fill in the circle next to your answer.**

7. **Todd . . . *blank* . . . aside his feelings of worry and stood up to bat. Fill in the circle next to your answer.**

8. **Heather helped me . . . *blank* . . . some of my lost books. Fill in the circle next to your answer.**

9. **My sister played her . . . *blank* . . . in music class. Fill in the circle next to your answer.**

10. **Rob is . . . *blank*. He invents so many clever things. Fill in the circle next to your answer.**

Record the student's score on the Word Reading Chart on page 95.

Part Four Concept Vocabulary

Make sure the students are on page 93. Begin by saying

- **I will read a number and the definition of a word.**

- **Fill in the circle under the word that best matches the definition.**

Pause after each item to allow students time to mark their answers.

11. **Fill in the circle under the word that means "delays or puts off until a later time."**

12. **Fill in the circle under the word that means "to have reached a goal or won success."**

13. **Fill in the circle under the word that means "the act of moving to a different country."**

14. **Fill in the circle under the word that means "the layer of gas that surrounds Earth's surface."**

15. **Fill in the circle under the word that means "a device used for observing objects in space or faraway objects on Earth."**

Record the student's score on the Word Reading Chart on page 95.

Name _____

Creative Caleb

When Caleb asked for a new bike, his father   9

suggested that Cal find a job. But what kind of job   20

could he get at his age? "Be creative," said Dad.   30

Caleb went for a walk. His neighbor, Mr. Drew,   39

was leaning down on the ground beside his porch.   48

"My kitten is in an awkward spot," Mr. Drew told   58

Cal. "I dread trying to get her out." Cal volunteered   68

to crawl under the porch and get her. "I appreciate   78

that," said Mr. Drew and gave Cal a tip.   87

Mrs. Smith came to watch. She needed to go to   97

the store, but she was too busy. Cal offered to go.   108

"Keep the change," said Mrs. Smith.   114

Cal was getting an idea. He would help people   123

with their errands. Caleb devised a plan. He made   132

flyers and put them in his neighbors' doors. Soon   141

the calls started coming in, and Caleb had a good   151

occupation. Cal's creativity paid off. By the end of   160

the summer, he had a new bike too.   168

© Pearson Education D

Unit 6 Test Passage

Comprehension

Directions Answer the following questions about the passage you just read.

1. What did Caleb want at the beginning of the story?

_____

_____

_____

2. What did his father suggest he do?

_____

_____

_____

3. What events helped Cal get his idea for making money?

_____

_____

_____

4. What do you think Cal wrote on his flyers?

_____

_____

_____

5. How was Caleb's work like a regular job? How was it different?

_____

_____

_____

Phonics Words

1. deal   dread   broad
    ○   ○   ○

2. understood   understand   underweight
    ○   ○   ○

3. scout   scold   scope
    ○   ○   ○

4. dial   duet   diet
    ○   ○   ○

5. creative   criminal   creamery
    ○   ○   ○

Phonics Sentences

6. Let's _____ the picnic blanket here.

    ○ spread

    ○ sweater

    ○ weather

7. Todd _____ aside his feelings of worry and stood up to bat.

    ○ whoosh

    ○ brook

    ○ pushed

8. Heather helped me _____ some of my lost books.

    ○ behind

    ○ child

    ○ find

9. My sister played her _____ in music class.

    ○ violin

    ○ riot

    ○ diary

10. Rob is _____. He invents so many clever things.

    ○ invaded

    ○ invention

    ○ inventive

Concept Words

11.   circumstances   procrastinates   devised

        ○   ○   ○

12.   perseverance   furious   achieved

        ○   ○   ○

13.   immigration   occupations   barrier

        ○   ○   ○

14.   atmosphere   propulsion   supersonic

        ○   ○   ○

15.   galaxy   scientific   telescope

        ○   ○   ○

Word Reading Chart for Unit 6 Assessment

Administer the Individual Test or the Group Test, not both.

Test Option 1 — Individual Test				
Phonics Words Circle the items the student missed.	**Total Items**	**Items Correct**	**Reteach**	**Retest**
1. Syllables with Short *e* Spelled *ea* *thread, health, feather, instead, sweatshirt*	5			
2. Syllables with Vowels *oo* in *foot*, *u* in *put* *crook, nook, cookbook, bush, cushion*	5			
3. Syllables with Long *i: ind, ild;* Long *o: ost, old* *unkind, mildly, older, scold, poster*	5			
4. Syllables V/V *create, liar, poem, radio, variety*	5			
5. Related Words *relate, relative, relationship, press, pressure*	5			
Phonics Words Total	**25**			
Phonics Sentences	**Total Items**	**Words Correct**	**Reteach**	**Retest**
6. Syllables with Short *e* Spelled *ea* *spread*	1			
7. Syllables with Vowel *u* in *put* *pushed*	1			
8. Syllables with Long *i: -ind* *find*	1			
9. Syllables V/V *violin*	1			
10. Related Words *inventive*	1			
Phonics Sentences Total	**5**			
Concept Vocabulary	**Total Items**	**Words Correct**	**Reteach**	**Retest**
11. *circumstances, conviction, model, procrastinates, devised*	5			
12. *hurdles, perseverance, achieved, furious, personality*	5			
13. *immigration, barrier, occupations, awkward, appreciate*	5			
14. *atmosphere, propulsion, supersonic, efficient, gauges*	5			
15. *telescope, galaxy, universe, futuristic, scientific*	5			
Concept Vocabulary Total	**25**			

Word Reading Chart for Unit 6 Assessment

Administer the Individual Test or the Group Test, not both.

Test Option 2 — Group Test				
Phonics Words Items 1–10. Circle the items the student missed.	**Total Items**	**Items Correct**	**Reteach**	**Retest**
Syllables with Short *e* Spelled *ea* Items 1, 6	2			
Syllables with Vowels *oo* in *foot*, *u* in *put* Items 2, 7	2			
Syllables with Long *i: -ind,* Long *o: -old* Items 3, 8	2			
Syllables V/V Items 4, 9	2			
Related Words Items 5, 10	2			
Phonics Words Total	**10**			
Concept Vocabulary **Items 11–15**	**Total Items**	**Items Correct**	**Reteach**	**Retest**
procrastinates, achieved, immigration, atmosphere, telescope	5			
Concept Vocabulary Total	**5**			

- **RECORD SCORES** Use this chart to record scores.

- **RETEACH PHONICS SKILLS** If the student is unable to read words with particular phonics skills, then reteach the missed phonics skills.

- **PRACTICE CONCEPT VOCABULARY** If the student cannot read tested concept vocabulary, then provide additional practice.

- **RETEST** Use the same set of words or an alternate set for retesting.

Scores for Subtests: Individual/Group				
	Phonics		Concept Vocabulary	
	Ind.	Group	Ind.	Group
100%	30	10	25	5
80%	24	8	20	4
60%	18	6	15	3

Benchmark Readers

> The Benchmark Readers may be used
> - to measure fluency (WCPM)
> - to evaluate comprehension (retelling)

To assess fluency and comprehension, you can use the activities that follow with the Level D Benchmark Readers. You also may use the Benchmark Readers to assess a student's mastery of phonics skills for a completed unit, using connected text. For your convenience, the Level D Benchmark Readers are reproduced on pages 97–111.

Level D Benchmark Readers

Unit 1: *Sharing Time*
Unit 2: *The Performers*
Unit 3: *Taylor's Secret*
Unit 4: *The Polar Bear Mystery*
Unit 5: *Jamal Flies*
Unit 6: *Not Just Another Move*

Assess Fluency Take a sample of the student's oral reading of the Benchmark Reader.
- Refer to page 10 for a detailed description of fluency assessment.
- Have the student read aloud for one minute. Record the words correct per minute (WCPM) on the Fluency Progress Chart, page 11.

Assess Comprehension Have the student read the Benchmark Reader quietly. If the student has difficulty reading the narrative, you may read it aloud.
- When the student has finished reading or you have finished reading aloud, ask questions about the story. Questions should be based on the narrative retelling criteria (see the prompts on page 12).
- Use the Narrative Retelling Rubric on page 12 to evaluate the student's retelling. Record scores on the Retelling Progress Chart, page 14.

Also for your convenience, the Benchmark Readers for Level C are reproduced on pages 112–123. For information about using Level C Benchmark Readers for placement, see pages 18 and 21 in this Assessment Book.

Level C Benchmark Readers

Unit 1: *How Rose Got a New Clock*
Unit 2: *A Squirrel's Story*
Unit 3: *The Good Deed*
Unit 4: *Hike in the Woods*
Unit 5: *Three Friends*
Unit 6: *Twister Free*

Sharing Time

"We all have special things about us," 7
Miss Benson tells the children. "Thursday you will 15
all share something about you that is special." 23

The children think about what they should 30
share. They all have different ideas. But they have 39
one idea in common. Each one wants to share 48
something that the class will like best. 55

Joe cannot decide what to share. He looks 63
at the pennies he has collected. They fill several 72
boxes. His classmates might gasp at the hundreds 80
and hundreds of pennies. 84

Or he could take the reptile skin he found on 94
a hike. Which thing should he choose? 101

Lisa looks around her room. She knows there 109
are many things that make her different. But 117
she doesn't know what to take to class. Should 126
she take the trombone her dad gave her? the 135
baskets she wove at camp? Which object will her 144
classmates admire most? Lisa rethinks her ideas. 151

Eric likes making people laugh. He could tell 159
his classmates a funny tale. Last week Eric tripped. 168
His glasses fell off and landed on his dog's nose. 178
Everybody would laugh at that. 183

But Eric decides to bring his new trumpet. 191
He has only had one lesson on it. He hopes his 202
classmates don't laugh at him when he plays it. 211

Level D Unit 1 Benchmark Reader

Hannah thinks. She could show her 217
classmates the rug she is making. But it is 226
incomplete. She could take her fossil bone. But she 335
does not know much about it. 341

Hannah thinks some more. Everybody knows 347
that she loves ants and wasps. But they don't 356
know that she has an ant farm. 363

Hannah discusses the idea with her mom. 370

In class the next morning Miss Benson hears 378
the children discuss their desire to share the best 387
thing. She dislikes this idea. 392

"Class," she says. Everybody stops to listen. 399

"This is not a contest to win. It is about 409
connecting with one another. It is about sharing 417
something about ourselves. Then we can see how 425
we are alike and different." 430

"Let's work together," Lisa says to Eric. "Our 438
classmates will hear what we can do with our 447
trumpet and trombone." 450

"Great!" says Eric. 453

"Let's work together," Joe says to Hannah. 460
"We will tell others why we like to collect things." 470

"I can't wait to show everybody my ant farm!" 479
says Hannah. 481

Miss Benson smiles as the children discuss 488
their plans. 490

The Performers

"There is nothing to do," whined Maria for the 9
thirteenth time that morning. 13

Her twin sister Carmen ignored her. Maria's 20
whining was endless. 23

"I am so bored. This is the dullest place on Earth!" 34

Carmen had heard Maria say this many 41
times. Now Carmen closed her book and looked at 50
her restless sister. 53

"What would you like to do?" Maria asked. 61
"We could go outside. Or maybe Grandma would 69
help us bake cookies?" 73

Maria was never silent. She never sat still. She 82
squirmed wildly on the sofa. 87

"Maria," Carmen said, "I have a great idea." 95

"What?" Maria asked in a hopeless tone. 102

"Let's put on skits. We can write the lines. We 112
can get costumes and props from the attic. We can 122
organize and direct skits. Then we can perform 130
them." 131

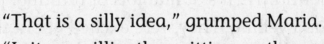

"That is a silly idea," grumped Maria. 138

"Is it any sillier than sitting on the couch 147
and whining? We can ask our friends to help," 156
Carmen said. 158

Carmen asked her friend Bill to help her. She 167
thought he was funnier than most comics on TV. 176

Maria asked her friend John to be her partner. 185
He was a skillful artist. He was sure to have 195
good ideas. 197

The attic was crammed with junk. It was a 206
great place to explore. Wonderful things lurked in 214
the darkness. 216

The children pulled out worn shirts, purses, 223
and scarves for costumes. They dragged out old 231
pots and dishes for props. 236

Then they sat down to write the lines for 245
their skits. 247

Carmen and Bill used the story of *Little Red* 256
Riding Hood for their skit. An old purse was the 266
picnic basket. A blanket was Red Riding Hood's 274
cape. 275

Bill was the Wolf. He was very funny. 283
Bill was a great sneaky wolf. Carmen moved 291
gracefully on the stage. Her long cape swirled 299
around her. 301

Maria and John based their skit on *King Arthur* 310
and His Knights. Their set was a king's throne. 319

Maria was a knight. John was King Arthur. 327
John made a coat of armor out of cardboard for 337
Maria. Their skit had lots of running, jumping, 345
and yelling. They were excited about their skit. 353

After dinner the children performed the skits 360
for their families. When they finished, everyone 367
clapped loudly. It was a very successful event. 375

Later that night, Carmen and Maria were in 383
their beds tired from their busy day. 390

"That was a lot of fun!" Maria said. "So, what 400
are we going to do tomorrow?" 406

Taylor's Secret

Taylor slowly stirred his oatmeal. His mother   7
was reading the newspaper.   11

"Mom," said Taylor, "today's the class trip."   18

"Yes, I know," said Mom.   23

"I can't go. It may rain, and I forgot where   33
I put my raincoat."   37

Mom said, "The paper says it'll be sunny   45
today."   46

"I think I lost the permission slip."   53

Mom said, "I put it in your backpack."   61

"I have a stomachache, and I may throw up."   70

Mom lowered the paper to look at Taylor.   78

"Why don't you want to go on the class trip?   88
What's the *real* reason?"   92

Taylor couldn't look at her. He mumbled,   99
"It's a stupid trip."   103

"Taylor Lee Gaines, stop acting like a   110
preschooler. The trip is prepaid, and you're going."   118

After lunch Taylor and his classmates arrived   125
at the nonprofit Needles Nature Center where a   133
volunteer greeted them.   136

"I'll be showing you some of our animals,"   144
Joan explained. "People bring us sick or injured   152
wild animals, and we try to heal them. If we can,   163
we'll release them back into the wild. If we can't,   173
they'll stay here with us."   178

Joan stopped next to a cage. 184

"This beaver had a mishap with a trail bike," 193
she said. "See its oversized front teeth? It uses 202
them to cut down trees. Beavers are amazing 210
builders." 211

The other children moved in closer. Taylor 218
remained at the back. He wouldn't admit it, but 227
he was a little afraid of wild animals. 235

Joan turned to the next cage. 241

"This hawk was struck by an arrow," she said. 250
"See its keen eyes? It's a good hunter. From high 260
in the sky it can spot a small rabbit far below in 272
a meadow." 274

The hawk suddenly flapped its wings. Taylor 281
could imagine the hawk sailing high overhead. 288
He moved a little closer. 293

Joan walked to another cage. 298

"This owl got its feet cut by some wire," she 308
said. "Like the hawk, it's a good hunter, but it 318
hunts at night. It can see as well at midnight as 329
the hawk can see at noon." 335

The owl's huge yellow eyes seemed to look 343
straight at Taylor. He moved closer. 349

At home Taylor talked nonstop about the 356
animals he'd seen. His mother was surprised and 364
pleased. She knew about Taylor's fear. 370

"I'm glad you had such a good time," she 379
said. "Maybe next weekend we can go to the zoo." 389

Taylor didn't answer. He was busy drawing a 397
picture of a hawk gliding high in the sky. 406

The Polar Bear Mystery

Bill and Joe noticed the sign at the entrance to   10
the zoo. The boys were at the zoo on a school field   22
trip. As junior detectives it was their duty to help   32
solve this mystery.   35

But first they needed to ask permission from   43
their teacher. She shouted, "Lunch. 12:00 o'clock.   50
Cafeteria. Be there or else!"   55

The boys arrived at the polar bear house. They   64
saw a woman spraying the polar bear boulders   72
with a hose.   75

"Excuse me, ma'am!" Bill shouted. "We'd   81
like to ask you a few questions!" The boys quickly   91
flashed their junior detective badges.   96

"Hey, I returned those movies last week!" the   104
woman answered nervously.   107

"No, ma'am." Joe said. "This is about the   115
missing polar bear."   118

"When was the last time you saw Scout?"   126
Bill asked.   128

"Last night," Zelda the zookeeper answered. "I   135
gave him two watermelons, and then I left."   143

Joe took out his notepad and pen. "What does   152
Scout look like?"   155

"White male, stands about six feet tall, and   163
has a long nose," Zelda answered.   169

"That sounds like half the people in this city!"   178
Joe exclaimed.   180

Zelda reached into her pocket and gave the   188
boys a picture of Scout. "This is Scout and I. I'm   199
the one cleaning the boulder," she said.   206

Bill noticed Zelda's black raincoat in the   213
picture. "How come you're not wearing your   220
raincoat?" Bill asked.   223

"I don't know what happened to it,"   230
said Zelda.   232

"Hmmm," Bill said. "We'll be in touch."   239

The boys studied their notes. Suddenly, Bill   246
stopped. "Look!" he shouted.   250

"Some litterbug threw snow-cone cups on the   257
sidewalk!" Joe yelled.   260

"No, not that," Bill said, pointing. "That!"   267
Black watermelon seeds dotted the sidewalk. "Are   274
you thinking what I'm thinking?"   279

"It's lunchtime?" Joe guessed.   283

"No," Bill said. "Those are watermelon seeds.   290
Follow the seeds and we find Scout!"   297

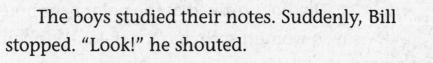

The boys followed the seeds all the way to   306
the entrance of Penguin World. It's where the   314
penguins lived.   316

Something wasn't right. A large group of   323
penguins was huddled together in the corner.   330
They looked frightened. They were shaking and   337
chirping loudly. And on top of the snow-covered   345
hill was the largest penguin the boys had ever seen.   355

"That's one huge penguin!" Joe exclaimed.   361

Bill looked closely at the large penguin that   369
was sliding down the hill. "That's no penguin!"   377
Bill shouted. "That's Scout!" Scout was wearing   384
Zelda's black raincoat and a snow-cone cup on his   393
nose. He looked just like a penguin . . . sort of.   402

"Let's go find Zelda! Another case solved for   410
the junior detectives!" Bill said.   415

Jamal Flies!

Jamal nervously looked down at the pavement. 7
Today he was taking his first plane ride. Ma and his 18
sister, Dawn, were going to nature camp. Jamal and 27
his dad were going to visit with Grandpa Floyd and 37
Grandma Joyce. They didn't have enough time to 45
drive, so they were taking a plane. Jamal was not 55
afraid of the farm, but he was a little nervous about 66
the plane ride! 69

"Ma," said Jamal, "I feel woozy." He looked 77
chalky and pale. As they walked to the car, Jamal 87
said to Ma, "My stomach is doing flips! 95

"Jamal," Ma said, "I know you are nervous 103
but I promise, you will be fine. You and Dad are 114
going to have a great time. I think you will like 125
flying through the air." 129

The airport was very busy and noisy. Jamal and 138
Dad waited with others to walk through the gate to 148
the concourse. 150

Dad asked, "Jamal, would you like something to 158
eat?" 159

"I don't think so, Dad," Jamal said. "My stomach 168
is still doing flips." 172

"Don't worry. I think you are going to enjoy 181
flying," Dad told Jamal. 185

Dad bought two sandwiches and some pretzels. 192
"You might change your mind," Dad said. 199

"Here's our gate; let's sit over by the window," 208
Dad said. 210

"Dad, is that the plane we are going to ride 220
on?" Jamal asked excitedly. 224

"Yes, it is," Dad said. "It is kind of a neat 235
invention, isn't it?" 238

"It is so big. How does it get up into the air?" 250
Jamal asked. 252

"The pilot will taxi out to the runway and 261
then speed up. Before you know it, we will be in 272
the air." 274

"Dad, I can't wait to get on the plane," 283
Jamal said. 285

"You may begin boarding the plane," a voice 293
said from overhead. 296

Dad said, "Grab your backpack; let's get on 304
the plane." 306

The friendly pilot greeted them as they walked 314
on the plane. 317

"We are so glad to have you on our flight," 327
the pilot said. "I hope you enjoy it." 335

Jamal and Dad found their seats quickly. 342

"Jamal, why don't you sit by the window?" 350
asked Dad. "You will get a better view." 358

Jamal watched the ground crew who were 365
busy preparing the plane for takeoff. 371

Dad said, "Look out the window; we are 379
passing through the clouds." 383

"This is really cool," Jamal said. "I can't 391
understand why some people are afraid to fly." 399

"Wow, the time flew by," Jamal said. "This 407
was a good choice of transportation, Dad." 414

They walked outside and found Grandpa 420
Floyd and Grandma Joyce. 424

"How was your flight?" Grandma Joyce asked. 431

"It was awesome," Jamal told her. "I am going 440
to be a pilot when I grow up, so that I can visit 453
you whenever I want." 457

"I am so happy to hear that," Grandma Joyce 466
told Jamal. "Let's go to the farm!" 473

Not Just Another Move

Diana took a deep breath. She was very upset 9 but wanted her voice to be steady when she spoke. 19

"When do we have to leave?" she asked. 27

"As soon as the house is sold," her father 36 replied. 37

"And the spaceship is ready," her mother 44 added. 45

Her brother, Leo, kept eating his breakfast. He 53 didn't mind another move but then he was only a 63 small child. It was different for Diana. 70

Mrs. Fuller was an inventor whose head was 78 full of creative ideas. She had invented ways to use 88 wool as fuel, make bread from mold, and control 97 bad weather. 99

Mr. Fuller was an engineer who made Mrs. 107 Fuller's wild plans into reality. He created the 115 machines that did the actual work. 121

Now their inventions would be used on Mars. 129 Mr. and Mrs. Fuller were very excited. 136

Mr. and Mrs. Fuller were already happily 143 making lists. Their pleasure made Diana bold. 150

She shouted, "You can't make me move again. 158 I won't do it!" 162

They stopped and looked at her as if she were 172 a two-headed creature. 175

"That is a childish remark," her mother said 183 mildly. 184

"There will be time for good-byes," her father 192 said kindly. 194

Diana ran blindly to her room. 200

The Mars colony was not that old. The first 209
colonists had arrived ten years ago. Today about 217
5,000 men, women, and children were spread 224
among the three settlements. They lived under 231
gigantic plastic domes. These protected them from 238
Mars's cruel climate and deadly air. When they 246
left the domes, they wore spacesuits with gold- 253
tinted helmets and dual air tanks. The people 261
looked sort of odd but no one seemed to mind. 271

Diana read all this and more on her hover 280
computer. Mars sounded dreadful. 284

Mrs. Fuller knocked softly and then entered 291
Diana's room. 293

"I know you want to stay here instead of 302
going to Mars, but we would miss you too much," 312
she said. "This will be a real adventure. Just like 322
the ones in your favorite video books. You may 331
like it." 333

Diana hadn't thought of the move like that. 341

"It will be only for a year or two at most. 352
Think of all the good stories you'll have when you 362
get back to Earth. After all, not many people have 372
gone to Mars." 375

That *was* a pleasant thought. Diana could 382
see herself holding people spellbound with her 389
incredible tales. 391

"Maybe moving to Mars wouldn't be too bad," 399
Diana thought. 401

Leo marched into the room. 406

"What are you guys doing in here?" he 414
demanded boldly. 416

His arrival ended Diana's daydream. She 422
sighed. She still dreaded the move, but her heart 431
didn't feel quite as cold and heavy. 438

"Let's find those lists. We have a lot to do if we 450
are moving soon," she told her mother. 457

Mrs. Fuller put her arm around Diana's 464
shoulders as they left the room. 470

How Rose Got a New Clock

Rose broke her clock. She dropped it outside. 8
This made Rose sad. She liked that clock a lot. 18
Rose picked up the pieces. But tape and string 27
would not hold them together. She could not fix 36
the clock. 38

Rose and Mom made a huge jug of lemonade. 47
She grabbed a bunch of plastic cups. She printed 56
"Lemonade Stand" on a big sign and hung it up. 66
She planned to sell the lemonade and use the 75
money to buy a new clock. 81

Calvin came over to inspect the lemonade 88
stand. 89
"Will you trade this stuffed frog for a huge cup 99
of lemonade?" he asked Rose. 104
Rose smiled and handed Calvin the glass. 111
Calvin gave Rose his stuffed frog. 117

Now Ellen is racing up to the stand. 125
"Will you trade these plastic sunglasses for 132
that stuffed frog?" she asks Rose. 138
Rose invites Ellen to take the frog, and Ellen 147
gives Rose the sunglasses. 151

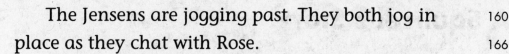

The Jensens are jogging past. They both jog in   160
place as they chat with Rose.   166

"Will you trade those sunglasses for this rabbit   174
cage with a cute stuffed rabbit in it?" they ask.   184

"Of course," Rose tells them.   189

Miss Teng stops and admires the cage.   196

"Will you trade it for a clock?" she asks. "It   206
runs well and has a nice face."   213

Rose laughs and nods her head. Miss Teng   221
rushes home and fetches the clock.   227

Rose is thinking about what happened. The   234
trades she made helped her get the new clock she   244
wanted. The next time Rose sets up a stand, she   254
intends to print "Sell <u>or</u> Trade" on her sign instead.   264

A Squirrel's Story

Amy the squirrel lived in an elm in the forest. 10
Her nest was perched on a branch at the top. It 21
swayed in the wind. 25

Then during a storm, the wind tore Amy's nest 34
apart. She tried not to cry about it. Now she must 45
build a new home. 49

Perhaps, Amy thought, she should visit other 56
homes to get ideas. Why did her friends live in 66
those places? What if one of them was a better 76
home for her? 79

Amy scrubbed her gray fur, curled her tail 87
over her back, and scurried away. 93

Helen the frog lived on a lily pad in a sunny 104
pond in the center of the forest. 111

"My home has plenty of flies and other bugs 120
for me to catch!" exclaimed Helen. 126

Helen's home was the wettest, muddiest spot. 133
Amy wanted a neater, drier home. 139

Jason the cricket lived in a crack in a stack of 150
bricks at the back of a garden. 157

"My home is hot and dry," Jason chirped. "I 166
can stretch out and sing." 171

Amy squinted into Jason's home. It was too 179
stuffy. She wanted a windier place. 185

Roger the skunk lived in a large hole under a   195
pile of stones by the forest border.   202

"My home is safe, and I can forage in the   212
forest after dark," explained Roger.   217

Roger's home was the draftiest place. Amy   224
wanted a snugger home than that.   230

Edith the snail was not hard to find because   239
she left a trail of sticky slime.   246

"My home is the shell I balance on my back,"   256
Edith replied. "I carry it with me."   263

Amy stroked Edith's shell. It was too snug. She   272
wanted a more open home.   277

Amy squatted by the elm to think. Her friends'   286
homes were perfect for them. But they felt very   295
strange to her.   298

"Bricks, stones, shells, and pads are not   305
squirrels' homes. I will stay in my elm and build   315
the biggest, grandest nest ever."   320

And Amy started that very day.   326

The Good Deed

Dean and his beagle Peanut are outside   7
playing in the backyard. Suddenly Peanut starts   14
howling at the willow tree.   19

"What do you see, Peanut?" Dean asks as he   28
peeks up in the huge green willow tree.   36

High in the top branches he spies—   43
"That's an eagle!" Dean shouts.   48

Mom is puzzled by the sight of an eagle this   58
far south. Clearly it shouldn't be here.   65

"We'd better coax it down," Mom says.   72

She and Dean bring out birdseed and sprinkle   80
it on the ground. Blackbirds fight eagerly to eat   89
the seed. The eagle flies to the top of an oak tree at   102
the next house.   105

Plainly Coach Reed doesn't feel grateful that   112
an eagle can be seen in his oak tree.   121

"It's not right. But I'll handle this," he   129
grumbles as he tapes a big net to a pole.   139

He leans out of an upper window and tries   148
to sweep the eagle in the net. It quickly flies to a   160
beech tree on the street.   165

Three men struggle to put a ladder by the   174
beech tree. But the ladder isn't long enough. The   183
eagle is at least 30 feet up.   190

By now there's quite a crowd around the beech   199
tree. Everybody thinks he or she knows best how to   209
deal with the eagle. Meanwhile, it has flown to a   219
maple tree.   221

The daylight is fading. How will they be able   230
to see the eagle without light?   236

"I'm getting more help," says Mom.   242

Firefighters arrive with a ladder truck. One   249
firefighter gets close and tries to put a coat over   259
the eagle. But it won't allow that and flies off.   269
Everybody groans loudly.   272

Next Mom contacts an animal expert.   278

"Please don't make a single sound," Lee says   286
firmly to the hopeful crowd.   291

He jiggles a chunk of meat on a string. The   301
eagle pounces on the "live" meal. Lee throws a   310
towel over the eagle's head and gently ties its feet   320
with silk cord.   323

The eagle struggles just a little bit.   330

Lee says, "He's weak because he hasn't eaten.   338
You've done a good deed. He might have died if   348
you hadn't helped."   351

Dean is thankful that the eagle will survive.   359
Maybe one day he'll see it, well and grown, flying   369
free in the skies.   373

Hike in the Woods

Jimmy pulled his sweater over his head. He 8
looked for his cap. He had misplaced it last night. 18
Jimmy found it under his bed. 24

At last, he was dressed and ready to go. He 34
ran to get Mom. Every weekend, they went for a 44
hike in the woods. Jimmy liked hiking, and Mom 53
seemed to enjoy it too. 58

Mom knows a lot about the plants and 66
animals. On their hikes, Jimmy would point to 74
trees. Mom would name them. "That's an oak. 82
This is a maple." 86

This morning, the cloudless sky was bright 93
blue. "It's a perfect day," Jimmy said. 100

Mom put on her sunglasses to block out the 109
brightness. Then Jimmy picked a trail. They began 117
to follow it. 120

At the brook, Jimmy took off his boots and 129
socks. He climbed on a rock on the shore. He 139
slipped a little and began to slide. Jimmy grabbed 148
for Mom. "Help!" he shouted. 153

Mom quickly helped him regain his footing. 160
Jimmy didn't end up in the water, but his cap did. 171

Jimmy looked unhappy, but Mom came to the 179
rescue again. She used a stick to pull the cap out 190
of the brook. Jimmy wrapped it in a towel and put 201
it in his backpack. 205

Then Jimmy sat down to put on his socks and 215
boots. He saw rocks that formed a pool. In it were 226
a few fish. 229

© Pearson Education D

118

"Look, Mom! These fish are no bigger than my thumb," Jimmy exclaimed. 238 / 241

"Those are tadpoles, not fish," Mom said. "Tadpoles are baby frogs." 248 / 252

"But, Mom, frogs are tailless," Jimmy said. "These tadpoles have long tails, and they are legless. Frogs have legs." 259 / 267 / 271

"True, Jimmy," said Mom. "Tadpoles do not look like frogs. But they grow and change. See these tadpoles. They are getting legs." 278 / 287 / 293

"As tadpoles grow, their tails get shorter and shorter. They grow legs. Soon, they can spend time on land and in water." 301 / 309 / 315

"Ribbit! Ribbit!" 317

Jimmy stood still. "What was that?" he asked. 325

"A frog," said Mom. "Listen. Maybe we can locate it." 333 / 335

"Ribbit! Ribbit!" 337

"See it, Mom! It's on that log. It's a big one. Look at it flick at the gnats." 348 / 355

"Yes, it is eating the gnats. Frogs eat insects," Mom noted. 364 / 366

"Yuck! I'm glad I'm not a frog," Jimmy exclaimed. 374 / 375

"I'm glad you are not a frog too. I wouldn't like cooking bugs for your dinner," she laughed. "Speaking of eating, it's time that we get home and make lunch." 385 / 393 / 402 / 405

"Ribbit! Ribbit!" Jimmy laughed, and so did Mom. 412 / 413

Level C Unit 4 Benchmark Reader

Three Friends

Justin, Paul, and Phil are eight years old. They   9
have been friends for a long time. They have lived   19
next to each other since they were babies. They   28
are in the same third grade class. They are on the   39
same soccer team. They are alike in lots of ways.   49
They are different in some ways too.   56

"Paul," his mom called. "It's time for dinner."   64
"Great, my grandma is visiting us. She made   72
my favorite dinner," Paul said. "She makes the   80
best egg rolls."   83
"What are egg rolls? Are they good?" Justin asked.   92
Paul thought for a second, "Wait here. I have   101
a great idea."   104
Two seconds later he reappeared.   109
"Go ask your moms if you can stay for   118
dinner," Paul yelled.   121

Phil asked, "Where are the forks?"   127
Paul said, "No forks tonight."   132
He passed out chopsticks.   136
Paul's grandma showed them how to use   143
chopsticks.   144
"Your grandma is a great teacher," Justin told   152
Paul.   153
"You are right, Paul. Egg rolls and rice are   162
good," Justin said.   165

"Can you come to my house for dinner next?"   174
"Justin, what is your mom making for   181
dinner?" Phil and Paul asked.   186

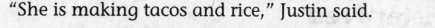

"She is making tacos and rice," Justin said.   194

"But we had rice last night," Paul said.   202

"She makes a different kind of rice. Just wait   211
and see. You will like it." Justin smiled.   219

Justin's mom showed the boys how to make   227
a soft shell taco.   231

She helped them fold the soft shells. Justin's   239
dad gave them some rice on the side.   247

"Is the rice hot or mild?" asked Paul.   255

"Don't worry, it is mild," Justin said.   262

Justin's mom asked, "Did you like the tacos   270
and rice?"   272

"It was really good," Paul said. " I liked it."   281

Next, the boys went to Phil's house. "My dad   290
has been cooking all day. You are going to love   300
it!" Phil told his visitors.   305

"What did he make?" asked Paul.   311

"He made sauce and pasta," Phil informed them.   319

Phil's mom scooped pasta into the bowls.   326
Then she poured sauce on top of the pasta.   335

His dad taught the boys how to twirl the pasta   345
using a spoon and fork.   350

"This is really good. I like pasta," Justin   358
announced.   359

"This has been a fun week," Justin said.   367
"We tried new foods."   371

"Every dinner was really good. But I am   379
stuffed. I can't eat anymore," Paul added.   386

"We are alike in lots of ways," Phil said.   395

"We are different in lots of ways too,"   403
Justin said.   405

"That why we're friends," Paul said.   411

"It's good to be friends!" they all agreed.   419

© Pearson Education D

Twister Free

Spring brings bright sunshine to the Midwest, where my home is. But spring can also mean thunderstorms. Thunderstorms brew up quickly and can bring twisters too. These twirling funnel clouds can be dangerous.

One day last spring, Mom was planting the garden. I had just returned home from my baseball game. I gave Mom my postgame report and then went inside for a snack. That was in the morning when the sky was a deep blue. By midday, though, it had changed and became a gray mass of dark storm clouds.

Mom came inside. "Turn on the television or radio," she told my sister Jen. "Let's get some up-to-date weather information. I think a big storm is likely. Dark, gray clouds are racing across the sky, and the wind is blowing hard."

Jen clicked the remote. "Storm watch for Lake and Cook Counties," the reporter noted. Then he gave some good prestorm advice. "Seek shelter. Do not stay outside. Do not stand by windows. Do not be caught unprepared."

As we listened to the report, the rain began. At first, just drops fell, but then it came down in buckets and beat against the windows. Then I heard a loud wailing sound. "What was that?" I asked.

Mom explained, "It's the town's siren, which is sounded when there's a likelihood of a twister."

7
16
21
29
33

40
49
57
67
77
85
91

99
108
117
126
132

140
148
155
164
169

178
189
197
205
207

215
223

122

At school and home, we had learned about 231
twisters. We knew we had to seek protection. The 240
best place to find that was the basement. Jen and I 251
didn't need much encouragement to move quickly. 258
We knew the possible danger. We ran down and 267
looked for a place to hide. Mom advised us to 277
get under Dad's bench. "It's a good, solid piece of 287
furniture," she said. "It will help protect us." 295

I scurried under it and Jen and Mom followed. 304
We huddled together. Windows began to rattle. 311
The noise got louder and louder. It sounded like a 321
train was speeding past the house. Jen whimpered. 329
I felt like crying too. But I tried to be brave. Mom 341
hugged us tightly. Then it was quiet. 348

Slowly we crept out and looked around the 356
house. To our amazement, it was in perfect shape. 365
We ran outside and looked up and down the road. 375
Everything looked undamaged. Late afternoon 380
news reports explained that conditions had been 387
right for a twister but one never formed. 395

Since that day, we have paid close attention to 404
storm watches. Mom said that last spring's storm 412
was the only time she thought that we would have 422
a twister. We are lucky. Our town has been free of 433
twisters for as long as Mom can remember. 441

Answer Key

Placement Test, pp. 20–23

1. Word Reading: Phonics

shack, drove, fifth, sketch, flute, comment, cactus, product, hundred, impress, shake, tadpole, confuse, invites, translate, pinches, asking, bodies, intended, scrubbed

2. Word Reading: High-Frequency Words

family, every, people, their, different, laugh, machine, picture, clothes, important, above, should, change, leave, beautiful, heard, country, build, special, America

3. Fluency and Comprehension

Assess Fluency

(Record the words correct per minute.)

Assess Comprehension

• *Who is the story about? Tell me more about these characters.* Mack, Jackie, and the person telling the story; Mack and Jackie can juggle balls, and the narrator wants to learn to juggle.

• *Where and when does the story take place?* In a park downtown "the other day," when the two friends are juggling

• *What happens in the beginning of the story?* Mack and Jackie each juggle three balls in a park. *in the middle?* The person telling the story asks the friends to show how to juggle, and they do. *at the end?* The two jugglers try to juggle four balls; the person watching hopes to learn. Evaluate using Narrative Retelling Rubric on p. 21.

4. Word Reading: Benchmark Words

gnat, search, midnight, preheat, chemist, instead, violent, applaud, daughter, overjoyed, shrewdly, cruiser, signature, reservation, neighborhood, decision, governor, additional, cheerfulness, intelligent

Unit 1 Test

Individual Test, pp. 24–26

1. Fluency and Comprehension

Assess Fluency

(Record the words correct per minute.)

Assess Comprehension

• *Who is this story about? Tell me more about Ann.* Ann, Kim, and Kim's mother; Ann learns to explore a cave.

• *Where or when does the story take place?* In a cave when Ann goes cave exploring for the first time

• *What is the problem or goal?* Ann doesn't know about exploring caves and is a little scared. *How is the problem solved or the goal reached?* Ann goes into a cave and forgets her fear as she sees the great views. Evaluate using Narrative Retelling Rubric on p. 12.

2. Phonics Words

1. fossil, pencils, zigzag, pilgrim, hundred
2. reptile, costume, suppose, escape, excite
3. happens, catches, foxes, buddies, spies
4. gripped, planning, skimming, ducked, stamping
5. unbutton, replace, dislike, disconnect, inside

3. Phonics Sentences

6. I gave a basket of plants to my mom.
7. Did Jill invite Mike to the picnic?
8. Miss Smith has a kitten and five puppies.
9. Sally hummed a tune I like a lot.
10. I felt unlucky when I lost my red socks.

4. Concept Words

11. ethnic, culture, homesick, translated, backgrounds
12. pioneers, perspective, territory, confused, voyage
13. route, journey, views, itineraries, transportation
14. arid, frontier, carved, canyon, guide
15. eruptions, astonishing, gigantic, unbelievable, naturally

Group Test, pp. 27–33

1. Fluency and Comprehension

Assess Fluency

(Record the words correct per minute.)

Assess Comprehension

1. Spelunking, or exploring caves
2. They loaned her supplies (hiking boots and hardhat with lamp) and told her how to be safe.

3. Before, she was unsure and scared; inside, she forgot her fear and enjoyed the views.

4. Rock formations, a small stream, and hundreds of sleeping bats

5. Possible answer: Caves aren't scary; they're exciting places to visit.

2. Phonics Words

1. sudden 2. escape 3. candies

4. shocking 5. replace

3. Phonics Sentences

6. basket 7. invite 8. puppies

9. hummed 10. unlucky

4. Concept Words

11. culture 12. perspective

13. itineraries 14. canyon 15. gigantic

Unit 2 Test
Individual Test, pp. 36–38
1. Fluency and Comprehension

Assess Fluency

(Record the words correct per minute.)

Assess Comprehension

• *What is the selection mostly about?* How people train whales

• *What is important to know about training whales?* Students may mention trainers getting to know the whale, rewarding it for jumping, and giving a signal to jump and a reward.

• *What did you learn from reading this selection?* Students should mention facts and ideas from the selection about training whales. Evaluate using Expository Retelling Rubric on p. 13.

2. Phonics Words

1. garlic, harvest, ignore, popcorn, important

2. thirsty, circus, serpent, perfection, hamburger

3. paler, tamest, snappier, sillier, stickiest

4. camel, vivid, salad, pony, event

5. suddenly, hopeful, closeness, sadness, timeless

3. Phonics Sentences

6. Herman liked the story about the old fort.

7. James felt the stiff whisker of a kitten.

8. Linn's ladder is safer than mine.

9. It is a short bike ride to our local park.

10. My sister walked slowly along the shore.

4. Concept Words

11. horizons, exhibit, interactive, experience, comprehend

12. collaboration, members, accomplished, orchestra, cooperate

13. inspiration, fantastic, skillful, extraordinary, sculptures

14. career, option, contribution, energy, workers

15. capital, executive, museum, dedicated, memorabilia

Group Test, pp. 39–45
1. Fluency and Comprehension

Assess Fluency

(Record the words correct per minute.)

Assess Comprehension

1. How people train whales

2. Gently force it to sit, say sit, and reward the dog with treats.

3. Possible answers: Get to know the animal; find out what the whale likes.

4. Like: communicating and rewarding the animal for actions. Different: Trainers do not force or hold the whale, and the rewards are different (such as squirting with water).

5. Possible answers: It wants to please a trainer; it's happy to learn.

2. Phonics Words

1. garlic 2. thirsty 3. stickiest 4. event

5. helpful

3. Phonics Sentences

6. story 7. whisker 8. safer 9. local

10. slowly

4. Concept Words

11. comprehend 12. collaboration

13. extraordinary 14. career 15. museum

Unit 3 Test
Individual Test, pp. 48–50
1. Fluency and Comprehension

Assess Fluency

(Record the words correct per minute.)

Assess Comprehension

• *What is the selection mostly about?* The Northern Lights

• *What is important for you to know about the Northern Lights?* Students may mention information from the selection: where the lights are seen, what they look like, the folk tale about them, or the way the sun causes the glow.

• *What did you learn from reading this selection?* Students should mention facts and ideas from the selection about the Northern Lights.

Evaluate using Expository Retelling Rubric on p. 13.

2. Phonics Words
1. portray, Saturday, claim, dainty, complain
2. be, beehive, seeded, treason, peaceful
3. don't, won't, aren't, she'll, we've
4. oatmeal, boastful, growth, showcase, snowflake
5. mistreat, nonstop, overflow, prepaid, midseason

3. Phonics Sentences
6. Daisy didn't explain the problem to me.
7. Rain streamed over the rim of my hat.
8. Joan doesn't want to go sailing on the boat.
9. Steve toasted his dinner over the campfire.
10. Let's eat the grapes before they get overripe.

4. Concept Words
11. equinox, solstice, calendar, lunar, calculate
12. observe, zones, shelter, refuges, nocturnal
13. rotation, vacation, hemisphere, revolution, unpredictable
14. phenomenon, inland, tsunami, behavior, coast
15. hydrogen, solar, benefits, resources, electricity

Group Test, pp. 51–57
1. Fluency and Comprehension
Assess Fluency
(Record the words correct per minute.)
Assess Comprehension
1. The Aurora Borealis, or Northern Lights, colors in the night sky
2. Unlike street lights, they are in the sky, looking like curtains of different colors, constantly changing.
3. They told a tale about an arctic fox that started fires with its tail, and the Northern Lights were the reflections of the fires in the snow.

4. Gases from the sun travel to Earth in a solar wind, which crashes into Earth's magnetic field, creating electricity and a glow in the sky.
5. The explanation about the sun, Earth, and electricity is scientific.

2. Phonics Words
1. daily   2. beehive   3. don't   4. showplace
5. misspent

3. Phonics Sentences
6. explain   7. streamed   8. doesn't
9. toasted   10. overripe

4. Concept Words
11. lunar   12. refuges   13. rotation
14. phenomenon   15. benefits

Unit 4 Test
Individual Test, pp. 60–62
1. Fluency and Comprehension
Assess Fluency
(Record the words correct per minute.)
Assess Comprehension
• *What is the selection mostly about?* Harry Houdini, a magician
• *What is important for you to know about Harry Houdini?* Students may mention that Houdini was famous, escaped from handcuffs and locked boxes, and created illusions.
• *What did you learn from reading this selection?* Students should mention information from the selection about Houdini.

Evaluate using Expository Retelling Rubric on p. 13.

2. Phonics Words
1. rattlesnake, handcuffs, tabletop, cannot, yardstick
2. high, might, lie, flying, why
3. chuckle, handle, purple, bundle, jumble
4. shouts, counter, south, thousands, how
5. glamorous, diver, explorer, joyous, actor

3. Phonics Sentences
6. We cannot go outside today because it is raining too hard.
7. The eagle soared high in the sky.
8. The belt had a big gold buckle.
9. A loud noise scared the sleeping dog.
10. The brave explorer reached the top of the mountain.

4. Concept Words

11. invisible, illusion, perception, vanish, magician
12. instinct, response, sense, young, protect
13. creative, discovered, treasure, solution, solve
14. conversation, symbols, dialect, combine, region
15. scrutiny, evidence, convince, diver, explorer

Group Test, pp. 63–69
1. Fluency and Comprehension

Assess Fluency

(Record the words correct per minute.)

Assess Comprehension

1. Students may mention that Houdini was a famous magician, escaped from handcuffs and locked boxes, and created illusions such as a vanishing elephant.
2. Tables cannot really float.
3. Making an elephant seem to disappear and a rabbit appear in a hat
4. He became famous for fooling people, making them "see" things that did not really happen.
5. They are alike as illusions that surprise people. Differences: The rabbit trick is small and makes a thing appear; the elephant trick is large and makes a thing vanish.

2. Phonics Words

1. underground   2. might   3. handle
4. south   5. glamorous

3. Phonics Sentences

6. cannot   7. high   8. buckle   9. loud
10. explorer

4. Concept Words

11. vanish   12. response   13. solution
14. dialect   15. evidence

Unit 5 Test
Individual Test, pp. 72–74
1. Fluency and Comprehension

Assess Fluency

(Record the words correct per minute.)

Assess Comprehension

• *Who is this story about?* The crew of a submersible craft (submarine) called *Alvin*

• *Where or when does this story take place?* In the submarine before and during an underwater expedition in the ocean
• *What is the problem or goal? How is the problem solved or the goal achieved?* A swordfish attacks the craft, damaging its skin. *Alvin* is hoisted to the surface.
Evaluate using Narrative Retelling Rubric on p. 12.

2. Phonics Words

1. moist, broil, poison, joyful, toyshop
2. union, mention, station, vision, picture
3. moose, scooter, threw, jewel, value
4. sidewalk, always, August, sprawl, slaughter
5. girlhood, statement, ashen, creaky, stormy

3. Phonics Sentences

6. Joy hoped the noise would not annoy her classmates.
7. The class discussion helped Roy understand the lesson.
8. Jenny saw a dentist when she lost a tooth.
9. My sister's cough woke me up every hour.
10. We stared in amazement at the heap of silver coins.

4. Concept Words

11. aquarium, isolated, oxygen, artifacts, destroyed
12. civilization, society, ancient, statue, traditions
13. dangerous, profession, expeditions, wilderness, adventure
14. adapted, burrow, extreme, prairie, homesteaders
15. craters, satellite, myths, mission, astronaut

Group Test, pp. 75–81
1. Fluency and Comprehension

Assess Fluency

(Record the words correct per minute.)

Assess Comprehension

1. A submersible craft for exploring underwater in the ocean
2. Oxygen for the crew, robot arms, camera equipment, and lights
3. They peered (looked) out the windows.
4. The attack caused minor damage in *Alvin*'s skin; the swordfish died (and was eaten).

5. Most students may say the crew would die because they were deep in water; others may say they would be rescued (same reason).

2. Phonics Words

1. boil   2. potion   3. crew   4. sprawl
5. creamy

3. Phonics Sentences

6. annoy   7. discussion   8. tooth   9. cough
10. amazement

4. Concept Words

11. aquarium   12. statue   13. expeditions
14. adapted   15. astronaut

Unit 6 Test
Individual Test, pp. 84–86
1. Fluency and Comprehension

Assess Fluency

(Record the words correct per minute.)

Assess Comprehension

• *Who is this story about? Tell me more about Caleb.* Caleb is a boy who wants a bike, and his father suggests he find a job.

• *Where or when does the story take place?* In Caleb's neighborhood during the summer

• *What is the problem or goal? How is the problem solved or the goal achieved?* Caleb wants a bike and needs a job to get the money; he does errands, people pay him, and he gets a bike.

Evaluate using Narrative Retelling Rubric on p. 12.

2. Phonics Words

1. thread, health, feather, instead, sweatshirt
2. crook, nook, cookbook, bush, cushion
3. unkind, mildly, older, scold, poster
4. create, liar, poem, radio, variety
5. relate, relative, relationship, press, pressure

3. Phonics Sentences

6. Let's spread the picnic blanket here.

7. Todd pushed aside his feelings of worry and stood up to bat.

8. Heather helped me find some of my lost books.

9. My sister played her violin in music class.

10. Rob is inventive. He invents so many clever things.

4. Concept Words

11. circumstances, conviction, model, procrastinates, devised
12. hurdles, perseverance, achieved, furious, personality
13. immigration, barrier, occupations, awkward, appreciate
14. atmosphere, propulsion, supersonic, efficient, gauges
15. telescope, galaxy, universe, futuristic, scientific

Group Test, pp. 87–93
1. Fluency and Comprehension

Assess Fluency

(Record the words correct per minute.)

Assess Comprehension

1. A new bike
2. Find a job (and be creative)
3. He helped get a cat out from under the porch for a neighbor who tipped Caleb, and another neighbor paid him for going to the store for her.
4. Possible answer: Need errands run? Caleb can help at low cost. Call today!
5. Like regular jobs, Caleb's job requires hard work, and Caleb's job pays. Differences: His work came from many people, depended on calls, and was different each time.

2. Phonics Words

1. dread   2. understood   3. scold   4. diet
5. creative

3. Phonics Sentences

6. spread   7. pushed   8. find   9. violin
10. inventive

4. Concept Words

11. procrastinates   12. achieved
13. immigration   14. atmosphere
15. telescope